A KIND OF INITIATION

An Autobiosophy

Robert Chamberlain

RB
Rossendale Books

Published by Lulu Enterprises Inc.
3101 Hillsborough Street
Suite 210
Raleigh, NC 27607-5436
United States of America

Published in paperback 2014
Category: Memoirs/Life History
Copyright Robert Chamberlain © 2014
ISBN : 978-1-291-91961-5

Acknowledgements

With gratitude to my wife, Judith, for her helpful suggestions concerning fluency and diction, and to my daughter, Hannah, regarding technical and design matters.

CONTENTS

A labyrinth is not a maze,
A common confusion.
There are no dead ends, no false ways
That a gleeful demon leads you on.
Sure, when you're in the middle of it,
That's how it seems.
But viewed from above,
The tantalising glimpses of the goal
And the sudden swinging away,
The going forth and the doubling back,
Are all subtle rhythms of the soul
That pulsate on its journey
To the heart of things.

Preface

It was the deaths of my two eldest brothers within a month of each other last year (2013) that made me realise how many questions I had about family history, which could not now be answered. Having recently crossed the age threshold of three score years and ten, I thought that perhaps I ought to set my life down in writing, for the sake of any curious descendants! Around that time also, I began to feel the need to bring more clearly to consciousness, the various hidden threads of meaning which I had sensed had woven the 'fabric' of my life. That's why I have invented the word *autobiosophy*, to indicate the intention to discern the working of Wisdom (*Sophia*), the 'Great Weaver', in one's life.

There's another reason why I wanted to write it. I feel the need to gratefully acknowledge certain people (if only to myself), who played an important part in my life even though many of them have subsequently gone their different ways. Without them, I would be a different person. This poses a fascinating question as to who we think we really are, - something working from within outwards or from without inwards.

I think everyone has a tale to tell. I have been told some extraordinary life stories in my time, far stranger and richer than many a novel. But they don't get written down. And those who consider they have led fairly 'ordinary' lives, might discover if they dig down deep enough, that even they have a unique record of that particular fragment of the world they have inhabited, which is worth sharing. There just need to be plenty of chroniclers to help those who don't have the confidence or the ability to write it themselves. If nothing else, it's a good creative and therapeutic exercise for those well on in years!

'Reality' is not out there, separate from our experience of it. Every time a language dies, a unique view of the world dies with it. So it is with individuals.

I feel like the producer figure which you find in some medieval Mystery plays who pleads at the beginning for the audience's indulgence for his company's rough and simple craft. What follows may not be piece of writing that would hit the best sellers' list, but it could be regarded at the very least as a spiritual and social document of the 1950's and 60's!

Before beginning my narrative, I just would like to mention some of the questions that began to arise as I started thinking about the whole project. How reliable is one's memory? I have checked as far as possible with family and friends and particularly in regard to childhood have allowed feelings to be evoked by my diaries, old photos and various sounds and smells. (Particularly evocative are the sounds of cuckoos and crows and the smell of fresh hay and cow parsley!)[1] How does one choose what to include and what to leave out? Can one find emblematic themes or motifs that somehow express the essence of particular episodes in one's life? A host of tempters appear before the soul, – to put oneself in a more positive light than one actually

---

[1] I wrote two poems some years ago about memory. See **Appendices 1** and **2**

deserves; to imaginatively elaborate and exaggerate certain episodes and incidents to make them more interesting to the reader; or to describe and interpret the past in the light of the awareness one has now, rather than how one saw things then. I was pleased to think of these pitfalls before a mischievous literary friend of mine, when he heard I was writing my life story, gave me a pie chart of the contents of a typical memoir, which he had cut out from The Guardian. *"25% - artistic licence; 20% - rose-tinted nostalgia; 17% - myth-making; 15% - verifiably true; 13% - possible but not likely; and thinner slivers of misremembered details, dubious memories, disputed facts, libellous score-settling and bullshit"*!

If that's true, I shall try hard not be the typical memoir writer! Except I do own up to being a myth-maker – 100%! But not as a Guardian journalist would understand a myth. For me a myth is not the opposite of fact but a making visible the archetypes that give it significance and meaning. We are all heroes in our own mythology.[1]

---

[1] If you just want the short version, skip to the Epilogue!

Introduction

Let me begin with a little 'counter-factual' imagination. This mental exercise of imagining 'what if' in our lives can heighten the sense that things had to be the way they were. Or to quote *Hamlet, 'There's a divinity that shapes our ends, rough-hew them how we will'.*[1]

If it hadn't been for two traitors, I mightn't have been born (at least in my present form!). One was beheaded in 1491 for betraying his King and Country. The other was hung in 1946 for being a mass murderer. The former was an ancestor of mine – Sir Robert Chamberlain. The latter, a traitor to the human race, was S.S. Kaltenbrunner, leader of the S.S in Austria.

In January 1491, Henry VII sent 140 troops to St. Cuthbert's sanctuary in Hartlepool and flushed out Sir Robert, High Sheriff of Suffolk, his two sons and eighteen accomplices. (A law had been passed allowing sanctuary to be broken in case of treason). They were suspected of getting ready to set sail to Flanders to join Perkin Warbeck, who was planning to invade England to claim the throne. Warbeck claimed to be Richard of York, one of the two Princes in the Tower. He had somehow escaped to France, and by some ten years later had managed to build up a band of followers who

---

[1] Distinguished actor, Ian Richardson, taking a stroll in the lanes around Stratford, back in the 60s or thereabouts. Meets two men trimming the hedges. Has a chat. Asks them, *"But tell me, why does it need two of you?"* Answer, *"I rough hews them, and he shapes the ends".*

believed his story. On Tower Hill, March 1491, Sir Robert aged 47, was beheaded for high treason. His sons and accomplices were pardoned.[1]

If Sir Robert had kept his head, I might well have not been born. But because he supported the lost Yorkist cause of the pretender, he was branded as a traitor, and after his execution his family estate and title were forfeited for all time.[2] If that had not happened it would have been passed on to his direct heirs, one of whom would have been my father, Leonard Chamberlain, over 400 years later. As the first in line, his responsibility would have been to look after the estate.[3] In which case it would have been highly unlikely that he would have gone on to train as a priest, study at Cambridge and to meet there an Austrian fellow student who introduced him to his sister, my mother...

* * * * * * *

If it hadn't been for an uncharacteristically charitable act of one of Austria's worst mass murderers, I might

---

[1] An interesting account of this strange period in English history is given in Ann Wroe's book, *The Perfect Prince.*

[2] Astutely, Sir Robert's widow married the man who was granted ownership of Gedding Hall, so she moved back in!

[3] The family mansion, Gedding Hall is now in the hands of a somewhat different sort of rebel,-Bill Wyman, ex- Rolling Stone. When I asked if I could look around, his lodge keeper very firmly declined the request. I wonder if ex-President Clinton and Princess Diana would have received the same treatment if they had asked, which they might well have done. It is said Sir Robert Chamberlain was Clinton's 14-great grandfather and Princess Di's 16-great grandfather.

not have been here to tell the tale. S.S Kaltenbrunner (which literally means 'cold well'), friend of Adolf Eichmann, was found guilty of war crimes and crimes against humanity at Nuremburg and hanged in 1946. It is said that towards the end of the war when he became one of Hitler's closest associates, even Himmler, his boss, feared him. In 1939, when war broke out, he was the leader of the S.S in Austria.

In the summer of 1939, my mother with her family of four sons was visiting her parents in Linz, as she did nearly every year since she married my father. He would usually join them later, but this year he didn't, because of the worsening political situation. Mother and her family were due to return to England at the beginning of September, but war was declared against England on the 1st of September and the borders became closed. It looked likely they would have to be interred as enemy aliens. Fortunately, a friend of my mother's family, a Mr Langoth, intervened on their behalf. He knew Kaltenbrunner from their schooldays at the Linz Gymnasium, (the grammar school which my uncle also went to, at about the same time) and appealed to him to allow this English family to return to England, saying that the father was a non-combatant, being a priest, and possibly arguing that they would only be a burden to the State. His response was, *I'm seeing my boss (Himmler) tomorrow in Berlin. I'll raise it with him.* The upshot was that some weeks later, my Grandfather received a document signed by Himmler, giving permission for them to leave. This my mother would have to show at the border.

The route back to England was a very complicated one. My four brothers, David (10 years old), Otto (8), James (4), John (2) and my mother (33) had to first travel to Berlin by train and then to Amsterdam, where they then boarded a plane to Copenhagen. They were very inadequately dressed in their summer clothes as winter was drawing in. While they waited for the next plane to England, Mother was able for the first time to contact my father. He had expected them to get a boat back across the Channel in September, and was distraught to hear that the ship was torpedoed and everyone on board was drowned. He could not get in touch with Austria to find out whether they were actually on it. Soon after this happened (and I recently learnt about this at my brother Otto's funeral), my father had a kind of spiritual auditory experience. A voice told him that he was not to worry. His family were still alive. This experience sustained him in the coming weeks until he heard my mother's voice on the phone. She and the boys would be flying to London in the next few days and my father was to meet them off the plane. But there was to be yet another ordeal for them all to go through. The plane caught fire just after they took off for London, and they had to immediately turn round and land back in Copenhagen. All the passengers managed to disembark safely. My brother James remembers being temporarily separated from the rest of the family in the rush to get off the plane, and then hearing the frantic calls of his mother, with whom he was safely re-united. Snow was falling heavily which added to the bleakness of their situation.

Soon they were all reunited and took the first train available to Gloucester and then a taxi to Sandhurst, a small village three miles away, where my father was the vicar. Four years later, in 1943 I was born, to be followed four years later by their first daughter, whom my mother was longing for...

* * * * * * *

Before embarking on relating my life journey, I would like to say something about the backgrounds of my parents and a little more about how they met. Father was born in 1900 to solidly middle-class parents who aspired to climb higher in the social scale. My grandfather was proud of the family tree that which had been traced for him - an expensive business in those pre-computer days. He was the editor of the overseas edition of the Daily Mail, and his father was the manager of a teetotal hotel in Norfolk. My father was the eldest of four sons, with one older sister whom later became divorced, a shocking fact that titillated us children. One brother became a doctor, another a minister of finance in the Gibraltar colonial government, and the youngest was sent down from Cambridge in disgrace, having got a girl 'in the family way'. He then emigrated to New Zealand.

My father seemed to be different from the others in that he didn't have any worldly ambitions. He was interested  in the big questions of life and Christianity seemed to be the best answer to them. This gave rise to the wish to become ordained in the Church of England. After doing his priest's training at Canterbury Theological College, he was sent to Fitzwilliam House at Cambridge to do a degree in Moral Sciences, which was really philosophy - consisting of a tripos in metaphysics, aesthetics and ethics. There he fully participated in the life of sport – rugby, cricket and rowing. (By the time I was born, he had given all that up and was leading a sedentary life). As I mentioned above, he became friends with an Austrian postgraduate, Otto Nicoleth, who after doing law in Vienna was pursuing language studies at the Sorbonne and Cambridge. They had lively discussions and arguments about philosophy and religion. Otto at that time was a convinced atheist. I remember him amusedly relating to me when I was studying philosophy myself, that my father then was excitedly trying to describe his latest philosophical enthusiasm, talking about the 'eelan vital'. Eventually my uncle realised he was meaning the 'élan vital' – the French word for the Life Force that Henri Bergson describes in his philosophy of Creative Evolution. Such was the ignorance of some educated Englishmen of the time and now, it has to be said. Otto on the other hand was fluent in several languages.

The story goes that my father visited him in his rooms and saw a photograph of an attractive girl on his desk. Learning that it was not his girlfriend but his sister, he immediately vowed he would meet her. He was convinced she would become his wife. Accordingly he got himself invited to Austria, and tried to woo her in English, as he couldn't speak German, and she couldn't speak English! Eventually communication got going with the help of a friend of hers who did the interpreting. After another visit and exchange of letters

meanwhile, the deed was done. Mother, - Olga, broke off her engagement to Walther Kastner, who later became one of the top lawyers in Vienna, and chose to join her life with an impoverished English clergyman, who had hopes of becoming a missionary to the Eskimos. They both wanted lots of children, which I suspect was the final deciding factor. Her Austrian fiancé had not been so enthusiastic about a large family. Mother's family was also solidly bourgeois. Her father was a bank director in Linz, a rather boorish character to all accounts.[1] Her

---

[1] He went to the same school, the Linz Realschule, as Hitler did years later. (Wittgenstein for a while was in the same class as the young Adolf).

I like to imagine that my Urgrossvater, (my grandfather's father) could have met Rudolf Steiner's father as they were both stationmasters in the Austrian Railways at the same time, which was then still a fairly small and new enterprise.

mother on the other hand was a rather refined and

 cultured lady who had finished her education at the hands of nuns in Ireland. Both parents doted on Otto because of his academic brilliance, and Mother felt she took second place in their affections. I suspect that
contributed to the fact that she was determinedly self-sufficient from a very early age. She didn't like holding hands as a child. I assume that must have changed as a young adult, otherwise it couldn't have been much fun for those who courted her! Her two passions throughout her childhood and adolescence were children, which took the form of dolls of all shapes and sizes, and gymnastics, which she excelled in. After leaving school, she trained as a children's nurse and that was when she met my father.

* * * * * * *

After my father had been a curate in East and then North London from 1927 to 1935, they then moved to Cheltenham where he was curate for another 2 years! They believed in a long apprenticeship in those days. (I don't know what happened to his dream of being a missionary to the Eskimos!) In 1937 they settled in Sandhurst, a village on the banks of the River Severn, near Gloucester, where he now had his own parish. By then they had four children.

On the 11th of September, at a quarter to three in the afternoon, in Gloucester Hospital, I came bawling into the world. Another boy. By this time Mother had stopped desperately desiring a girl. (My brother, John who was six years older than me, was, as an infant, dressed like a girl longer than what was considered normal). She was just glad this birth was successful. Two years previously she had had a miscarriage.

Apparently, along with a rather large head, I had quite pronounced Mongolian eyes, which I still faintly retain. There is a family rumour that way back, someone on my Mother's side had had a relationship with a Hungarian 'on the wrong side of the bedclothes'. So some 'Hunnish' blood could have been flowing down the generations!

For those interested in such things, my sun sign is Virgo, (the same as my hero Goethe's), my ascendant is Sagittarius and my ruling planet is Jupiter. I learnt all this when I was 40, when I had my chart done. On this date, the 11th of September, D.H. Lawrence and Arvo Part , and er...Bashar al Assad were born, the Beatles recorded their first single, *Love me do*, and of course *9/11* occurred, a birthday I shall always remember. (As the world tragedy unfolded, I was having to take a tenant of ours to hospital, who was suffering severely from alcoholism.)

My 'Golden Age' (1-9) [1]

Up until the age of nine, I lived in Sandhurst. It was an idyllic existence for a child. One could freely roam far and wide, down to the river or up the local hill. (One of my early memories, which was not so idyllic (!), was running down the hill with my playmates away from a charging bull. I was told by my brother that it was because I had a red waistcoat on, which was part of my beloved cowboy outfit. (I can still vividly recall the thrill of getting it on my birthday – the shiny pair of colt pistols with caps, the leather holsters, the sheriff's badge, the tasselled hat...)

The only serious restriction I remember Mother placing on me was that I had to be back in time for meals and for bedtime. I remember protesting how unfair it was that I had to come in from play on a summer evening on hearing the dreaded family whistle,[2] while the other children were allowed to stay out longer. But to no avail. It was Mother's rules and that was that. They had to be obeyed. She was strict but consistent. She administered the discipline in the family with sharp words. I don't remember being too much affected by it. It was just a fact of nature, like rain or wind. Here is a

---

[1] I explain on page 211 why I liken the different periods in my life to the various 'Ages'.

[2] 40 years later my wife and I still sometimes use it if we want to find out where the other one is, in say, a supermarket. More often now though, we use mobile phones.

poem I wrote for her funeral which expresses some of these sentiments. She died in 2003 when she was 97.

O Mother, dear Mother
You were like
A force of nature
An immovable rock
And a stream that flowed
A rain that dowsed
And a sun that shone

I might as well have blamed the rain
Or praised the sun
As to have blamed or praised
What you have done

You simply were
A fact before which
One stands, in love and awe

I think I prefer to remember you
As a tree that grew its roots
Deep into the earth
And spread its branches wide into the air
Nestling our young lives there

And now your soul-seed
Wings its way
Into the ethereal blue
Only to root itself eventually again
Into the dark, moist earth

My father, on the other hand, kept a fairly low profile. It was only for the more serious cases of misdemeanour that you were sent to him in his study. Being quietly reprimanded by him was far more upsetting than Mother's harsh scolding. (I'll give an example in my 'Silver Age' narrative). I remember him as a kind and generous man, with a good sense of humour.

Life was full of mysteries which could not be fathomed by my childish mind. One of them was the wondrous phenomenon of the church which miraculously disappeared behind the hill and then reappeared as we were driving past it. My brothers would cry out, *'Look, there's the disappearing church!'*

We lived in a rambling Victorian vicarage big enough for us family of eight. The age range of the children was spread out, with the oldest, David being 15 years older than me. Then came Otto, who was 13 years older, then James who was 9, and John who was 6 years older. Olga, the only girl, was 4 years younger than me. And then there was Helga, the Alsatian who was my age – a fierce-looking creature with a loud bark, but a peaceful nature. Though if they didn't know that, it couldn't have exactly been easy for visitors to enter the vicarage garden! We had chickens, which supplied us with eggs and meat, and for a time, some pigs and a cow called Daisy whose milk was hand churned into butter. This was Otto's responsibility, who later became a farm labourer in Wales. The garden was large, with a small orchard, and a lawn large enough to play tennis and croquet on.

According to our cleaner, Mrs Rawson, who lived in a little thatched cottage nearby, my first word was 'water'.

(I fondly imagine that was a remnant of my time as a disciple- probably a very lowly one- of the ancient Greek philosopher, Thales of Miletus, regarded by Aristotle as the first philosopher, who held that all things arise from water). Apparently I didn't speak much in the next few years. My brothers could see what I wanted without my bothering to ask. My first memory was asking a prisoner of war who was working in the road outside the vicarage to repair my tricycle, and he said he would, in return for a cheese sandwich which I duly got from my mother. I must have been no more than three, when there were still prisoners of war around in 1946. By the time I was four, I must have learnt a few words by then, including some choice swear words, for I remember shouting them from up a tree at the infant school at the other end of the playing field which adjoined our orchard, for not allowing me to go to school – a sentiment that was to be reversed in my teenage years! According to my mother I had tried to go with the other children to school but was sent home because I was not on the register.

My clearest memories of the Infants' School are of playground games such as hopscotch, the 'alley alley oo' and marbles, raffia, and being punished by Miss Williams for naughtiness, by having to sing *My Joyful Rover* in front of the class. The shame and embarrassment of it I can still vividly recall. The experience was only redeemed when a few years later I was asked to sing by myself *See Amid the Winter Snow* to an appreciative congregation in my Father's church during an evening Christmas service, with snow falling silently outside.

Life was filled with rhythms – the rhythm of days and weeks, - baths on Wednesdays and Saturdays, with hair washing and nail clipping vigorously carried out by Mother. This was an iron rule which one never thought of questioning! Every Sunday morning and evening I sang in the church choir for which I was paid sixpence, and dutifully attended Sunday school in the afternoon. If the electricity went off, which it did occasionally, I had to pump the church organ. My older brothers were bell ringers. The seasons were distinct and followed one another predictably – quite often snow in the winter, (according to the diaries I wrote when I was a little older), long sunny days in the summer, conkers in the Autumn, fog in November and frequent floods with the Severn overflowing its banks, which cut off the village from Gloucester. Christmas was the most magical time of the year. Leading up to it, we had to place on the window sill a list of presents we hoped Father Christmas would bring. If we behaved ourselves, the note would mysteriously disappear the next day. If not, it would remain there. A day or two before Christmas Eve, we were aware that Father had brought a Christmas tree into the house and put it up in the dining room. This was all done without our seeing it, and we couldn't get into the room as it was locked. One could only get a whiff of the tree through the keyhole. Handmade paper decorations were strewn around the house on Christmas Eve, with ample bunches of holly and mistletoe. The excitement increased. Mother would be baking cakes and biscuits; her bachelor brother, Uncle Otto, who came every year from Austria to be with us, would be endlessly smoking his Turkish cigarettes and getting merrier and merrier with the drink which seemed to be liberally flowing. The tipsier he became, the more annoyed my mother was with him. My father and brothers joined in the fun and gales of laughter rose along with the fumes of alcohol and the tobacco smoke, which included that coming from my father's pipe. When darkness fell, the ritual began.[1] Father would disappear into the tree room, and light the candles and sparklers on the tree. We would then hear the Christmas hand-bell rung three times by him – the first time was the signal for all of us to get ready, the second to line up in order of age outside the door, and the third to come in. The sight that greeted us was a glimpse of paradise-flickering, sparkling lights and the dim outline of a tree which tapered up to the ceiling. Everyone kissed and embraced, wishing each other a happy Christmas, then a carol would be sung and then Father would ask us to remember our loved ones, including those who had died. This could go on too long for us younger children who were dying to open our pile of presents. Then followed a meal of fish or Wiener schnitzel. The big blow-out was on Christmas Day itself. Then everyone apart from us two youngest children and Mother, went off to Midnight mass. The next day there was no opening of stockings. That English tradition was only added to the Austrian one in a modified form in our own families, when we had children. After the morning service would be the big meal of chicken or sometimes turkey, - quite a luxury in those days, - followed by Christmas pudding and nuts. Then the obligatory walk to work it all off, followed by

---

[1] I carried that practice on in my own family.

tea and homemade Austrian biscuits. In the evening there were games, - monopoly, chess, and charades, with liberal supplies of drink for the grown-ups. I remember Father's face getting redder and redder, his eyes more twinkly and his speech more voluble. His religious duties were all done and he could really let his hair down. The only other times I remember him like this were when we were on holiday in Austria. According to my brothers, he had a mischievous sense of humour and liked playing practical jokes. Once he and his brother-in-law, Otto, went to meet young Otto at the train station, dressed as Arabs, and concocted some outlandish tale about why they were meeting him off the train, instead of Father.

Another high point of the year was Easter, when an attractive young nurse, Jean, - the daughter of an old friend of the family- always came to stay. Her presence seemed to enliven the spirits of the Chamberlain household! She was keen on David, then Otto, but he fell for her best friend whom she brought one Easter, later in 1956. That led to their marriage and Jean emigrating to New Zealand. What was it about New Zealand that it became a destination for disappointed or shamed lovers!

The summer holidays seemed to stretch out endlessly, with day trips to Weston-Super-Mare in our little Ford 8 and occasionally two-week holidays in Rottingdean, near Brighton where Grandpa lived, or at the Clergy Rest Home in Clevedon, a holiday guest house for poor Anglican clergy families! Twice in this period, in 1949 and again in 51, the younger half of the family went to Austria by rail. (This was paid for by Mother's relatives).

The most vivid memories of my first trip when I was six, was first the discomfort of sitting on wooden slatted seats of the 3rd class railway carriage for a day and a night going there, and sitting on our suitcases in the corridor coming back. And the excitement of seeing the 'enemy,' the Russians, through binoculars, in their zone, just outside the city. Linz was just in the American zone.

My maternal grandparents had died a few years earlier; 'Grossvater' was run over and killed by a police car which mounted the pavement. Apparently he had always had a fear of being run over and was extra cautious about crossing the road. It was almost as if he had a premonition about how he was going to die. I learnt later that it was possible he was deliberately killed because he knew too much, as the bank director, about the misappropriation of Jewish funds that passed through his bank. If he had told the Allied authorities what he knew, the perpetrators would have been prosecuted. Like a lot of other 'decent' middle class citizens of Linz whose savings were wiped out by the crash of 1929, he became convinced that the Nazis would put the country back on its feet, which they did in the beginning. They saw the economic successes in Germany and when Hitler annexed Austria, they thought the same economic miracle would be wrought.

In the Linz museum today, near the Town Hall, from where Hitler addressed the crowds from the balcony, you can hear the recording of Hitler's speech. It is extraordinary listening to it today, to imagine people being taken in by his fanatical ravings which were so harsh and ugly in tone. There was one person I know who wasn't, then a young music student, who was a relative of my mother. He knew instinctively that he was a dangerous fanatic. He discovered later that his wife-to-be was also in the crowd, and she was initially convinced. It divided families and households throughout the city, although it seems the majority were in favour, at least to begin with. My grandparents' maid, a devout Catholic of peasant stock, knew he 'was up to no good'. My Uncle, being a judge, had to join the Nazi Party, but it was not by conviction. It was particularly difficult for him when war broke out and he was obliged to join the army, as his sister's family, whom he was devoted to, was on the enemy's side. Another terrible dilemma for him was that, already before the war, he felt he could no longer sit in judgement on homosexuals, as he himself was one. Under the Nazis, homosexual acts were regarded as a crime, punishable by death, so he had to be incredibly careful himself. It must have been with some relief that he found himself being a soldier on the Russian front, no longer being a judge and not fighting against the British. Having said that though, it must have been agony for him to have to be prepared to kill, as he was the sort of person who wouldn't harm a fly. He suffered the cataclysmic defeat at Stalingrad and those that survived, he among them, had to find their own way home. He was given a medal for turning back and helping an injured comrade to safety. Now after the War, he was recruited by the Americans to be an interpreter, which he continued to be until the Americans left.

Years later when I visited Austria in my twenties, it was very difficult to get people to talk about that time. It was like a bad dream which they wanted to forget. My uncle was traumatised by the whole experience. The apple of his parents' eye, he had had a brilliant legal career ahead of him. Overtaken by world events and his own sexual orientation, he gradually descended into alcoholism, only modified later by being able to visit our family in England once or later twice a year, and late in his life, conversion to Catholicism. I remember him as a warm-hearted loving soul with a playful sense of humour, and possessing a vast reservoir of knowledge. Given the damage he did to his liver, it was extraordinary that he lived as long as he did, until he was eighty.

* * * * * * *

Thinking back to my time in Sandhurst, it seemed I was different in character and temperament than later in my teenage years. Then I was much more of a leader – I was the boss of the vicarage gang, partly I'm sure because it was my garden! We had pitched battles against another village gang, throwing stones from up 'the climbing tree' in the corner of the garden near the road. We had two kinds of huts which we built ourselves, with a little help from my brother John, – an underground one with corrugated roofing on, and one constructed out of odd boards with sacks as lining, also with a corrugated tin roof. There we had an oil lamp and spent many happy hours in there doing I know not what! Except I do remember snogging a girl called Brenda while wishing I would rather be with Maureen, who was with my friend next to us on the bench! They say country lads and lasses are a bit more advanced than city ones, and vicars' children even more so. I blame it on the example set by my older brothers, particularly the two immediately above me, whose romantic goings-on must have filtered through to my childish imagination. More of this happened in my 'silver age'. In my 9 and 10 year old diaries, I wrote *'I heard James kissing his new girlfriend'* and *'John is in love with Pruscilla. John is 16, Pruscilla is 14. Much too young to love!!* That didn't seem to apply to me as underneath I wrote, *'Robert loves Sheila Brown. Sheila is 10, Robert is 9'*. Having older brothers around (the oldest two in the holidays) provided a backdrop of laughter and jokes, a lot of which was completely incomprehensible to me. About this time, Otto, the second eldest, who was a bit of a tearaway and a great concern to his parents, let off his shotgun to frighten James, his next younger brother, and his girlfriend, Peggy, who were merrily giggling outside his bedroom window after coming back late from the youth club. What with him firing his twelve bore occasionally out of his attic bedroom, a fierce-looking Alsatian who barked at anybody coming into the garden, and the vicar's wife with a funny foreign accent, and Austrian to boot, it was surprising that any parishioners dared to visit the vicarage! But they did. Apparently Father was a good listener and counselled countless people. Pastoral care was his forte, rather than the 'Hail fellow, well-met' vicar routine. Mother became a well-respected village matron who kept well out of parish affairs. Being in Sandhurst was the happiest time of her life. Later in his life, Otto became a very loving father to five children and a successful farming instructor to boys in a Borstal school!

Other vivid memories from that time was the sheer joy of making trucks out of boards and old pram wheels and tearing down the local hill, and transporting empty beer bottles which had been discarded in the ditches, to the local pub. We were paid a penny for each one. Another memory was the story of the ghost that haunted one of our attic guest rooms, next to the one where we played trains. Jean, the down-to-earth nurse who stayed with us often, scornfully dismissed such tales and said she would be happy to sleep in 'the ghost room'. Later that night she suddenly woke up and saw a black figure like a nun, at the end of her bed. I don't think she slept there again! Otto was the only psychic in the family (he was very good at water divining), and he often was aware of 'atmospheres' in that part of the house. Apparently, the cleaner, when she was a little girl, had looked back at the vicarage, which was empty at the time and saw a black-robed figure appearing in the attic window.

A word about what I remember enjoying reading – *Babar the Elephant* books which were large and colourful, *Rupert Bear*, *Winnie the Pooh*, and *Struwwelpeter*, Victorian morality tales, whose vivid illustrations of characters like *Harriet on Fire* who played with matches, or *Peter* whose long finger nails were clipped with shears, held a ghastly fascination for my young impressionable mind. There was of course no TV, but occasionally we were taken to the cinema. My first film was, I think, *Snow White and the Seven Dwarves*, and the one that made the most impression on me was *The Wizard of Oz*. My favourite radio programme was 'Children's Hour' with Uncle Mac, at 5 o'clock in the afternoon. Other passionate pursuits of that time were playing marbles, 'aggies' as they were called, conkers in the Autumn and playing cowboys and Indians. Making your own bows and arrows was a real art.

Although the War was over by the time I was two, the after- effects were still present. I remember when I was four or five, looking with horrid fascination at the only bombed-out building in the village, caused by an aeroplane dropping its last bomb while returning to Germany, after a bombing raid on Birmingham. Ration books, 'glass'-preserved eggs and the joy of eating our first bananas were all part of the times. Mother would tell us children, when we were older, how she was suspected of being a spy by some villagers, because she hung her washing up on Tuesdays, not Mondays, (Father had his day off then). They thought she was signalling to enemy aircraft. She was also apprehended as an enemy alien because she was noticed knitting in the continental manner. And this together with her pronounced Austrian accent (which her family always teased her about throughout her life) added to their suspicions. I suppose they must have been allayed by her explaining she was the wife of a local vicar! She also told us that David and Otto, my two oldest brothers, were spat upon as they cycled to Gloucester Grammar School during the War as they were known to have an Austrian mother.

When relatives, as relatives inevitably always did, asked me what I wanted to do when I was grown up, I replied, 'a naval chaplain'. I don't think I really knew what that was, but in my childish imagination, it was somehow a mixture of the fact that my brother Otto was  a sea cadet, my father was a priest and at that time I often wore a naval outfit, which little boys did in Edwardian times, a tradition that continued to exist in our family, strangely brought over by my mother from landlocked Austria, which used to have a navy in its Imperial days!

I suppose that if I were to choose an experience that I remembered from that time which could be regarded as a recurring theme with variations in the 'unfinished symphony' of my life, then it would have to be the following. Here was I, a cherubic-looking 8 year-old choir boy sitting in the vestry of my father's church before the service began. Next to me was Brenda, or was it Maureen, (?!) whom I was keen on at the time. I can still vividly recall the fresh smell and crisp texture of the white surplices we wore and the thrill of craftily sliding my arm down behind her, after first nonchalantly holding onto the handle of the safe behind us – the safe that contained the precious Holy Communion vessels. This I regard as an emblematic conjunction of the sacred and the profane, the sublime and the sensual, even if it was the relative innocence of a pre-adolescent! As Faust says in the play of the same name by Goethe which I directed over 25 years later, *Two souls alas reside within my breast, - the one to heaven soars, the other to earth is pressed.*

In 1952, we moved to another village, still in Gloucestershire, but nearer a town – Swindon Village near Cheltenham. Now the next phase of my life began.

My 'Silver Age' (9 to 11)

Swindon Rectory was not quite as large as Sandhurst Vicarage, but it had a big walled garden with a separate vegetable plot that my father worked in most afternoons. Now Father had two parishes to look after - a sign of the times, because of a declining number of churchgoers. Elmstone Hardwick was a small hamlet about three miles away, which to all accounts he preferred. Swindon Church and C. of E. Primary School were almost next door to us, and the neighbouring town, Cheltenham, was that much nearer and more accessible. From about ten onwards, I remember cycling into town with my mates, particularly to the Odeon cinema club on Saturday mornings.

The reason why I call this phase of my life my 'silver age' is that it feels, looking back, that clouds were looming on the horizon. After the sense of an almost continual paradisal present, and a space with no limits, I now felt time and space as pressing realities. The Intelligence Test and the 11-plus exams were inching ever closer, giving rise to anxiety and unease. If one failed them, one was cast into outer darkness, - to the Secondary Modern where the tough, rough kids went, or at best to the Technical School. Here began my exam phobia which was to plague me till the end of my university life.

A vague sense of forbidden pleasures began to seep into my blood stream in relation to girls. If I had been asked then why that was so, I'm sure I couldn't have given an answer. Two memories of that time stand out.

One was the episode with Sheila Brown, a local girl whom I went out with for a while. A local parishioner spotted us walking hand-in-hand down Lovers Lane (I learnt its name recently!). I can't remember doing much more – perhaps a bit of kissing. He reported it to my mother saying this was not what a vicar's son should be doing! Mother gave me a good telling off and sent me to my father in his study. While I was openly defiant with my mother, my father's quiet reprimand reduced me to tears and I promised I would never do it again. (I can't say that promise was kept too long!) The other memory was overhearing sniggering talk about girls by some older boys. I couldn't quite understand what they were on about. I had to wait another year when I started secondary school before I found out. One of my first memories of the new school was being told by an older boy and realising with a horrified fascination that the King and Queen do it! In those days there was no sex education by either the school or the parents. You had to learn it on the street.

Another very vivid memory of that time was hating injustice of any kind. One incident was to do with the school bully, whom I loathed. I can still remember his name – John Rone- and what he looked like, a thin, wiry boy with spectacles. One day, I challenged him to a fight when he ventured into our garden. I asked him to wait a moment while I went inside to change my clothes, but when I came back he had 'scarpered'! From then onwards however, he stopped bullying me. In my diary of the time, I wrote on 27/2/53, *John Rone asked if I would like to go tomorrow to his place for dinner and tea. I said Yes!* On the 28th I wrote, *I didn't go to Rone's stinking place. Went to Roderick's place instead.* It sounds like he was trying to be friends. But I was obviously having none of it!

1952 was the year that I first kept a diary, and this practice continued till I was sixteen. I still have them to refer to. Recording events and feelings in the flow of time through preserving them in writing, was obviously important for me, just as it was at a certain point in the history of humanity. A related practice was the taking of photos which I began with a brownie box camera. This also has the effect of making the temporary, permanent. A few years later I progressed to a German folding camera which my Austrian uncle had initially given to my brother, John, and I started carefully to compose shots of scenery and people, which I then developed and printed, following John's example.

Although life was gradually taking on a different hue, some things didn't change. I had a gang of friends, - we made huts, raced each other climbing up trees, and the rituals of Christmas and Easter continued. I still went to church - a good vicar's son that I was. New hobbies were taken up- making model aircraft and flying them, roller skating and above all, table tennis which we played almost every day at Colonel Smythes' mansion.

I said earlier that I remembered myself as somewhat of an extrovert when I was with people of my own age. In my 10 year-old diary I wrote down the names of my Robin Hood Gang. I was Robin Hood, and the infamous John Rone was Little John! However I do recall being quite quiet and reserved when it came to being with older family members and friends. One of them called me 'the philosopher' because it looked as if I was thinking and observing a lot without saying anything. It was probably more like common-or-garden shyness, which increased in my adolescence.

According to my Letts School Boys diary of 1953, which had separate pages for the books and films one saw, with a column for 'Remarks', I thought that *'Just So Stories'* by *Rudyard Kipling* were *'not bad'*, *Children of the New Forest'* by *Captain Morgan* was *'quite good'*, *The Children's Hour Annual* was *'good'*. But what capped them all was the remark of *'excellent'* for various Enid Blyton books about *'The Famous Five'*! So you can see the state of my literary appreciation then! (According to my 13 year-old diary, *Biggles* came top.). Films seen that year, *Road to Bali* with Bob Hope was *'poor'*, *Cruel Sea* was *'excellent'*, *Desert Legion* with Alan Ladd was *'super'*, and *Black Orchid* was *'good'*.

If I were to choose an episode of this time– an emblematic theme which weaves through my life's composition, then it would have to be the intense feeling of injustice that I had concerning the school bully – an experience that took on wider social connotations later on in life.

My 'Bronze Age' (11 to 14)

B efore I was eleven in September 1954, I had to take the entrance exam for Tewkesbury Grammar School. With some of my primary school class mates, I had passed the Intelligence Test and the 11+. Now there was this further hurdle. I remember coming out of the exam and saying defiantly through my tears to my father, *'I don't care if I'm not good enough to come here'*, thinking I had

made a bad job of it. But I got in. It was a small rural school with over two hundred pupils, with one class per year. I remember standing out from the others (which one desperately didn't want to do) because my mother had made the school blazer herself, sewing the light blue braid around a darker blue jacket. This was to save money. We were members of the 'genteel poor'! Although we lived in a grand house with a large garden, it was not our own. We were quite badly off compared to other professional middle-class families.

Father handed over a large part of his meagre parson's salary to Mother for housekeeping, and she had to make do with mending, patching and darning and never throwing food away if it could be turned into soup of some kind. Nothing else was discarded if it could be mended. (When my mother died at the age of 97, she still had tools that I remembered from my childhood, still in reasonable working order, and reclaimed nails and screws in various tobacco tins). Toilet paper was made of paper bags neatly cut to size with a string going through one corner and hung up. The ghastly medicated Izal toilet paper was kept for guests. A lot of my clothes were 'hand-me-downs' which I had accepted as a fact of life. However at this time, I remember becoming more self-conscious about how I looked, and when I was about thirteen, I wanted my trousers tapered in the Teddy boy fashion of the time.

I now became more aware of money, or rather the lack of it. Although my parents never had serious rows in front of us younger children, I do remember worry and anxiety about money seeping through their conversations. When James crashed the family car, a Ford Prefect which one of our wealthier uncles had given us, Father could not afford to replace it, and James, as a junior architectural assistant also could not. So my father bought a bike with a 'power pack', a small petrol engine on the back. It drove a small wheel which turned the top of the back wheel. It had an accelerator on the front handle bar like on a proper motor bike. I had great fun riding it up and down the rectory drive when nobody was looking. This got him to his other church for services. But for a time things got worse. To save petrol, he walked across the fields to his other church, which was about three or four miles away, and to find his way back in the dark, he shone his torch on balls of white paper which he had stuffed into bushes along the way.

Just before he died, in 1957, things must have got a bit better, because he bought a BSA 125cc motor bike, which I later inherited from David, my eldest brother.

Father was by nature a generous person, and spontaneously would take us for a treat, - a meal out or a visit to the cinema. Mother frowned on such impulses because I suppose she was all too aware of the state of the finances. I remember two occasions when he came to pay for something, he had no money. One was when I asked for my pocket money. Only a few small coins were shaken out into his tray purse, and I recall feeling quite sorry for him that he couldn't pay me then. The other time was when he took us all out to a restaurant and found out he didn't have enough money, which caused great hilarity on the part of my elder brothers. This was the time when I started to earn some money doing odd jobs mowing people's lawns, fruit picking and 'spud' picking up.

Apart from money worries, other dark clouds were piling up during this time. Mother had a serious operation concerning blood clots in her chest, and later Father had an operation for his sciatica. More seriously, he began to have angina attacks, for which he took medication. While out walking, he would suddenly slow down, and clutch his heart, and then out would come his pills. At first they happened only infrequently, and he seemed to make light of them, so I don't remember being too concerned. Nobody in the family, it seemed, realised how serious and life-threatening these attacks were. So it came as a great shock when he died.

It was when I was about eleven that I first became aware of John's epileptic attacks, for which he eventually had successful medication. He also suffered from acute psoriasis, and the combination of the various drugs that he had to take, caused serious side effects which eventually gave rise to severe arthritis later on in his life. On top of all that he suffered from hay fever, which I also did. I remember him having a volatile temper directed mainly against Mother, but he had an infectious enthusiasm for his various hobbies, such as photography, which rubbed off on me.

James suffered from asthma attacks, for which he had an inhaler; Otto occasionally from fits of depression, 'misuc moods', as he called them. Typically he was the joker in the family. Comedians are often melancholic at heart. I don't remember David having any serious ailments. Nor did Olga and I, apart from the usual childhood illnesses which at that time one was encouraged to get. Chicken pox, measles and whooping cough caused long stays in bed, which I liked despite the pain and discomfort, because it meant time off school and special treats and sympathy all round.

Apart from all the family worries about money and illness, I still remember it as a fairly care-free time. I was still mad about table tennis, roller skating, bikes, mucking about with the gang, making and flying balsa wood model aircraft, and courting local girls. One was Ann Williams who lived opposite. We seemed to have exchanged several love letters, according to my 1955 Eagle diary. Some were posted and others were by hand. What was in them I have no recollection! On the 5th May 1955, I wrote in my diary, *'Jill doesn't love JB any more'*. (John Brown was my best friend at the time). *Faithful Ann still loves me even though she's a friend of Jill'*.

I began to take up other hobbies – fencing, (the swords were given to me by my brothers); playing the guitar –an old, battered Austrian one from Mother. (Big Bill Broonzie and Josh White were my favourite blues guitarists); bell ringing - our church had five bells; and shooting an air pistol, which shot either lead bullets or little darts. I also began to take an interest in traditional jazz. My first records were of Louis Armstrong, Kid Ory and Chris Barber. Apart from occasionally listening to some of my eldest brothers' classical music records, I didn't take a serious interest until a few years' later. What did hit the Chamberlain household with a big bang was Rock 'n Roll, which was introduced by my brother John. He had bought a drum kit which he bashed out to a recording of Bill Haley's Comets over and over again, which didn't endear him too much to the rest of the family. James, the next eldest brother, loved hearing opera on the radio, so the two blared out in competition. In a way, the advent of rock 'n roll marked the beginning of youth culture which separated John from James. I remember being very wary of teddy boys who roamed the streets of Cheltenham. If you looked them in the eye, you were fiercely accosted with the remark, *'Wha' uh you lookin' at, mate?* Mumbling an incoherent reply, you stepped aside on to the road as they walked by, taking up the whole of the pavement. It was the time of luminescent socks, DA's (duck's arse, swept-back brylcreamed hairdos and chewing gum. I was more attracted to the Beat culture of jazz, dark glasses and polar-neck jerseys towards the end of this period in my 14th year. (A few years later came the added sophistication of existentialism and the poetry of Allen Ginsburg and Jack Kerouac!)

I listened to a lot of radio at this time, - mainly at night on Uncle Otto's old crystal set which afforded me the exquisite pleasure of finding a station with the mere twiddling of a knob, enabling a crystal to be tickled with a wire whisker. My favourite programmes were *'Journey into Space'*, *Hancock's Half Hour*, (which I still find funny) and *Paul Temple* – a detective series. I read crime thrillers and saw lots of war films, musicals like *'The King and I'* and epics like *'Gone with the Wind'*.

On the whole I enjoyed school apart from the increasing homework and exams. My position in the class fluctuated wildly from first to seventh depending on when the exams were. I remember with fondness and respect one or two teachers particularly - Jimmy the maths teacher, who was short and rotund like the comedian Jimmy Edwards, with a gravelly voice, probably due to the whisky he was seen tippling occasionally. He inspired me with a love of algebra and geometry, which I became quite good at. And then there was Tommy the Welshman, also short and stocky, who enthused us with his love of poetry, read out with a lovely lilting voice; and 'Girly' the music teacher whom everyone thought was a 'homo' because he wore suede shoes.

I also loved woodwork, which I had to give up when I was thirteen, because I was destined for the academic route – a dreadful division between the intellectual and practical skills which children still suffer from today, half a century later. When I was thirteen, I won a prize for reading - the only prize I won in all my secondary education, and I excelled for a short time in football when I played centre half in the junior school team.

Round about this time, Father took me to London for a few days and showed me the sights. We passed a second-hand camera shop and I saw a Pathé wind-up 9.5 ciné camera going for £5 and hesitatingly asked if I could have it. I was passionate about photography, but now I desperately wanted to do movies. Immediately he went in and bought it, which made me feel very ashamed, as I knew he was always hard-up. He must have realised that this would be the last treat he could give me, as I learnt years later that about this time his doctor had given him only months to live, a burden that he kept to himself until the last few weeks when he told my older brothers, and presumably my mother. Apparently, they refused to believe him, which I find impossible to understand.

On November 29th, not long before his 57th birthday on December 13th, he died suddenly from an angina attack. If it had happened a few decades later he would probably have survived, because by then bypass surgery had been developed. These new techniques saved the lives of John and Otto, who also suffered from heart problems when they were middle-aged.

For some years after his death, the smell of tobacco smoke and hearing Beethoven's Fourth Piano Concerto brought back vivid memories of him, and a deep feeling of sadness. He was not often seen without his curved pipe stuffed with Three Nuns tobacco. (The pipe cleaner paper holders made a good cigarette, filled with dried clover when I was a young lad!) Smoking surely shortened his life. And the aural reminder arose from the time, not long before he died, when I accompanied a couple of my brothers, who spent a considerable time in one of those listening booths in a record shop, comparing different soloists' interpretations of Beethoven's Fourth Piano Concerto. They eventually chose Solomon's version and bought it for his birthday, which was to have been a couple of weeks after he died.

My Father's death dramatically marked the end of this phase of my life. The two chief themes emerging out of this time, (and into my next phase) which continued to weave throughout my subsequent life, were the enigma of death and suffering, and the idealisation of the feminine. Of course the latter could be explained psychologically by the fact that being in a boys' school, girls were looked on as mysterious creatures! However I don't think it can be wholly reduced to that level of explanation. I like to think it was like an echo into this time, of the Medieval ideal of courtly love that the troubadours sang about, or like the Divine Feminine that Goethe describes at the end of his play, *Faust, Part 2*.

All that shall pass away is but a parable.
All insufficiency here finds perfection.
All that's mysterious here finds the day.
The eternal feminine show us our way.

My 'Dark Age' (14 to 25)
(Otherwise known as the *Iron Age* or *The Kali Yuga*)

This period of my life can be divided into seven phases. The first was the two years up to 'O' levels; the second was the time in the 6th form; the third was life at University; the fourth was my time in Germany; the fifth when I was in Austria; and the sixth and seventh during my three years in London.

1st Phase. Three months after my father died, we were found a council house on the other side of Cheltenham, on a housing estate in Shurdington. Now we were a family of three, - my sister, my mother and myself, and for the first time we two children had rooms of our own. By this time, my next three elder brothers, John, James and Otto were already engaged, and our father's death speeded up their decisions to get married. So within two or three months after the funeral, there were three weddings in succession, which certainly lightened the general family mood. David, the eldest brother, as I have already said, was working as an Anglican curate in Sheffield.

Not long after my father's death, David invited me to stay with him. His parish included a rough housing estate in Parson Cross. To give a flavour of how I was at the time, I will quote an excerpt from a letter I wrote back home to my mother (which I had found amongst her papers after she died). '... *Arrived at Sheffield at the scheduled time and David and guess who? – right first time! –my dear Sister Millicent* (meant jokingly)- *were there to pick me up.* And further on in the letter...*Sister M and David, - things are certainly developing.* It was family gossip that Sister Millicent, an Anglican nun, had a crush on him, as did quite a number of ladies even when he became a monk. I was evidently impressed by the parish work he and the other 'Fathers' did -(being a High Anglican church, they were called 'Fathers')- for I wrote, *'There's never a dull moment in this house. Everybody is on the go all the time. They never hardly sit down in the evenings, and when they do there's always somebody at the door or on the phone. "Please Farver, can we borrow your bike?"..."Can I 'ave a shilling for the gas?"... "'Ave you got a threepenny stamp, Farver".* And about David I wrote, *From what I've heard and seen, Father David is liked very much by all, in his unobtrusive and sincere way of doing things'.*

We went on a parishioners' walk on the moors and there I became acquainted with a girl called Susan, with whom I fell madly in love. Unlike my earlier adolescent dalliances, this was experienced almost like a religious ecstasy. I don't remember anything more than just holding hands when we went to a classical concert the next day, but I was so filled with gratitude that I went down on my knees when I prayed that night, thanking the Almighty for being so happy! In the remaining few days that I spent in Sheffield, we went for walks and boated on a lake. I never saw her again. All that I had to remind me of her was a rather blurred photo of her in the boat, part of which I enlarged so that I could have a close-up of her face.

* * * * * * *

I felt ready for change, and nothing my old headmaster could say, persuaded me to stay on at Tewkesbury Grammar, even though I had been reasonably happy there. Now I became a pupil of Cheltenham Grammar, a school four times as big, with four streams to each age. Presumably because I had been in the top five of my class in my old school, I was put in the A stream, but the boys in this class were a year younger than me. As they were rated as *'la crème de la crème'* of their year, they were doing their GCEs a year earlier. This meant for me somewhat stiffer competition than I had had in my old small rural Grammar school! Now I was consistently in the bottom five of the class. (I found my old school reports recently, and there's a dramatic change from being consistently good at everything, including science, at Tewkesbury Grammar, to being poor to average at Cheltenham Grammar).

I began to hate the whole ambience of the school. Firstly I felt anonymous being in a much larger one. Secondly there was much more relentless pressure to compete against your fellow students, whether in class or on the rugby pitch. Because I had a large build, I was put in the scrum, and inevitably got hurt. I did everything I could to get out of playing. As I began to realise later, they were aping the local public school, Cheltenham College, with having to wear mortar boards, at least in the 6th Form; its emphasis on sport and being persuaded to join the army or air force cadets, and making you feel inferior if you 'weren't the right material' for Oxbridge. There were lots of petty rules and regulations which I rebelled against and was as a result often put into detention, often by prefects who strutted around like petty dictators.

Reading my diary of the time, when I was 15, I'm surprised at how many times I skived General Science and PE and got away with it. Science was presented in such a dreary, factual way and PE was led by an ex-sergeant major whose brusque manner was too much for my sensitive adolescent soul! There was a small gang of us who sloped off to the Black Tulip, a coffee bar, or to the local cemetery for a quick fag.

I cannot remember any teachers that I really liked, apart from a young student English teacher. There were one or two whom one could respect but mostly they were either feared, loathed or ridiculed. There was one French teacher whose life we made a misery. He would shout himself hoarse, - his favourite phrase was '*You blithering idiots!*' A few years later I learnt that he suddenly died of a heart attack, which made some of us feel guilty.

My mother provided a stable home life with her predictable routines. Although it was a huge change of circumstances for her, from living in a large vicarage to being in a council house, I think she actually preferred it. She often remarked how she didn't like being isolated inside a walled garden and preferred seeing and being with 'ordinary people' (She always voted Labour). From being a practical and down-to-earth sort of person, she had no time for my earnest cultural pursuits! She would often interrupt my avid listening to the Third Programme as it was called then, with the remark, *Do we have to have that boring stuff on?* I would sigh and retreat to the kitchen which had a radio in it. I didn't have one of my own, but I did have a Dansette record player in my small bedroom which was a haven of retreat. On the brightly-coloured walls of orange, yellow and blue which I painted myself, were homemade wooden holders which displayed my jazz and classical LPs; a pin-up of Susan Hampshire who reminded me of Susan, the girl I fell passionately in love with in Sheffield; and a black and white reproduction of Raphael's *Madonna,* which accompanied me throughout my childhood, and which I had never thought of removing.

I did various chores around the house and garden, - drying up (she always insisted on doing the washing up), bringing in the coal, weeding, cutting the grass and sawing up branches of wood. These she used to drag behind her from various places in the village, tied on with old nylon stockings to the back of the bike she was riding. This was a Ladies Raleigh which was still in good condition after thirty years of use.

It couldn't have been easy for her, having her family, which had been the focus of her whole life, suddenly being reduced to three; and having to bring up two teenagers by herself. According to my brothers she allowed us much more freedom than she did with them. She found comfort and strength in her local church and in her beloved eldest son, who seemed to do no wrong. I didn't feel part of all that and this, looking back, heightened my adolescent's growing sense of apartness. I got on well with my younger sister Olga, by this time (Earlier she was mercilessly teased by me and her other brothers). She must have felt a terrible hole in her life without her father, whom she had doted on. We had our own circle of friends and we only got to know each other properly in our twenties.

We were not very well off. Mother had her widow's pension as well as her clergy widow's pension. I learnt later that my two eldest brothers helped out. Otto paid us two children's pocket money out of his small farm labourer's wage, and David the council rent out of his curate's salary.

I started piano lessons which I think a family friend paid for, gaining a grade-5 pass when I was seventeen. I continued with the guitar and took up the clarinet for a while and had occasional jam sessions with friends. The highlight of my week's entertainment was seeing on a Friday night, episodes of *The Third Man* and *Hancock's Half Hour* on next door's television. Mother was given a television after I had left home. (I remained a 'telly virgin' until I was 36, when I got married, and then the rot set in! My wife, Judith had brought with her a small black and white one which she had won at a raffle. It was kept under the stairs and only taken out at night when the children were in bed).

I don't remember at this time having any agonising doubts about Christianity. I still went to communion though not so regularly. I knew the words of the service by heart, which were etched into me from childhood. It was a slow drifting away from the church whose beliefs and practices just did not meet my emotional and intellectual needs. More on that later.

After getting seven 'O' levels (not including General Science, needless to say!), I was rewarded with a 6-week long holiday in Austria, which my Mother had arranged with her relatives and friends. This was like paradise! I drank and smoked, scrambled up mountains, swam in lakes, sailed on yachts, and met lots of pretty mädchen, without my usual agonised shyness. Compared to my dull and dreary life back in England, with all its emotional and financial restrictions, this was very heaven!

* * * * * * *

2ⁿᵈ Phase. Being in the 6th Form was a distinct change in my life. Everything began to be experienced more intensely. The constant pressure of completing assignments – I was studying English, French and History – gave rise to a continuing state of anxiety; my loathing for the whole school system increased. I cannot recall many occasions of having simply human, friendly conversations with any of the teachers. I was At War with the ethos of the school, the teachers, and the world at large! But now began an exciting journey of intellectual discovery which compensated for all this misery. Apart from the Romantic and Metaphysical poets that I was studying as part of the English syllabus which I loved, most of my discoveries were outside the school studies. Now at last there were thinkers and artists who could throw a light on the feelings of alienation and angst that pervaded one's life. Now one was not alone. One belonged to a secret coterie of fellow sufferers, no longer just a socially inadequate and disaffected teenager! There were three or four of us at school who felt superior to other students. We read the existentialists like Sartre and Camus, and felt like one of Colin Wilson's *Outsiders*. We ran a school magazine called *Schizoid* – we were the Aesthetes, others, - particularly the rugby-playing, science students were the Hearties, a distinctly inferior species! (At the time

C.P. Snow's *Two Cultures* debate was raging.) We dramatized T.S.Eliot's epic poem, *The Waste Land,* visited the Left Bank in Paris and sat in the *Café Les Deux Magots,* (ten years too late to meet any genuine existentialists!), smoked Gauloises and listened to modern jazz. However, in certain respects I felt like a double outsider because of the residue of Christianity that I still had, compared with other outsiders.

Pascal

Accordingly, I read Pascal and Kierkegaard - the founders of Christian Existentialism, Paul Tillich, Bonhoeffer and a book by John Macquarrie[1] about Rudolf Bultmann, a 20th century theologian, which 'demythologised' the traditional account of Christianity.[2] I remember being inspired to write a long poem about it which contained a lot of lengthy German philosophical words coined by Heidegger, who had influenced Bultmann. I was mocked by my unbelieving friends for its pretentiousness, probably justifiably so!

What I remember now of Pascal over fifty years later, was that he said that *the heart has its reasons which reason does not understand.* This is similar to a remark by Steiner, *In our day, the heart is beginning to have thoughts.*

---

[1] I was initially disposed towards Blair when he came to power because he claimed him as one of his main intellectual influences!

[2] I have to thank Eileen, Otto's wife, for giving me this book, along with a record of Eartha Kitt, which appealed to my more sensual side!

Kierkegaard

And what has stayed with me from studying Kierkegaard was his statement, *It is a positive starting point for philosophy when Aristotle says it begins with wonder, not as in our day with doubt.*

Again it was exciting for me to discover ten or so years later that Steiner had stressed the importance of cultivating a sense of wonder for gaining higher knowledge.

One question I was trying to formulate at that time was how to make sense of the reality of the Christian revelation without dogmatic assertions or institutional strictures[1] – to experience it in a free, authentic way (to use a good existentialist term). I believed for a start that the Anglican Church which I knew best, should disestablish itself, follow Lady Poverty in the Franciscan sense and rediscover the power of the interior life – prayer and mystical states of consciousness. (At the time I was learning about Eastern mysticism from reading Huxley's book, *The Perennial Philosophy*).

Christianity had to be *scandal,* not a comfortable bourgeois option, as Kierkegaard said. Otherwise we would have a false Christ as depicted in the Grand

---

[1] I learnt later that my father towards the end of his life had written down his thoughts about how the Church structures and practices should change. He wanted to abolish all the exotic ranks that had accumulated over the centuries like canons, deans, very reverends and most reverends etc, and just have curates, priests and bishops. Part of the day should be devoted to physical labour and there should be communal life centred at the cathedrals. I think he must have been yearning for a kind of monastic order which also allowed families, like the extended Essene communities in Palestine at the time of Christ.

Inquisitor', - an episode powerfully depicted in Dostoyevsky's *The Brothers Karamazov,* which had become my 'bible' at that time. Its main characters embodied in an archetypal way, aspects of myself and my group of friends that were warring against each other. One brother, Ivan was the intellectual cynic; Dimitri, the eldest was the sensualist; and the youngest, Alyosha, was the representative of the forces of purity and goodness.

Here I first began to be aware of the tripartite nature of the human being, which seven years later I found to be one of the basic concepts in Anthroposophy. We have physical bodies which give rise to our instinctual life; we have an inner life of feelings – our soul, and we have minds, our intellectual life. They are not three separate parts, but modes of being through which we connect to the world.

I was being taught to develop intellectual, analytical powers which repelled me and left me cold. (Paradoxically, of course, it was those very powers which awakened me to the state of mind I was in.) Warmth (or rather, heat) was to be found in a kind of compensatory reaction in the soul – the forces of sensuality. True heart warmth however was to be experienced in religious and aesthetic feelings that I also experienced as an opposing force to both physical passion and to intellectual cleverness. It was like being pulled in three different directions by these wild horses of the soul, and the rider was powerless to control them. Although I didn't articulate these feelings by using this kind of image then, that best describes the confusion I felt, and a growing awareness that 'the rider' must find a way of integrating these conflicting powers into a greater harmony of being. This was to be a kind of Grail Quest which I began to set out on. (Although *The Brothers Karamazov* was the book that meant most to me at the time, I was disappointed not to experience the same pleasure when I tried to read it again twenty or so years later. I now found it hopelessly exaggerated and fevered in its characterisations!)

One day I could be filled with spiritual ecstasy listening to my father's old 78 records of the Busch Quartet playing Beethoven's C sharp minor quartet, and the next, with sensual passion listening to a song by Julie London. Or I would be wafted into ethereal heights singing plainsong when I stayed at my brother's monastery. (By this time he had become a monk in the Community of the Resurrection, an Anglican Order in Mirfield, West Yorkshire). And the following week at a party, I would be jiving to modern jazz with a girl I would very much have liked to have gone to bed with. And the next day, I would be torturing my mind writing a history essay ready for Monday morning. Forget Michelangelo, - what about the Agony and Ecstasy of a disaffected teenager in the early sixties!

My relationship to girls at the time was fevered and fleeting. Because the school still held to the barbaric custom of being single-sexed, the opportunities of mixing naturally with them were simply not there. There were only the few times of having 6th Form dances with the girls of the neighbouring high school. Or one fervently hoped one would be invited to a Saturday night party, where one had the chance to meet other members of this exotic species, like some of the more liberated students of Cheltenham Ladies College, (one of them I remember was Lisa Jardine, eldest daughter of Jacob Bronowski), or the Art School, whose premises were above our school. Now began the habit of drinking alcohol to give one Dutch courage to talk entertainingly to girls. Unlike my boyish self, I was now hopelessly shy and introverted. Talking about existentialism was not exactly a turn-on! I was filled with loathing and envy at the superior confidence and ease with which boys from Cheltenham College, the local public school, managed to chat up girls with such trivial small talk. I was not like them. I had Significant Thoughts, but it didn't seem to get anywhere with the girls! I remember an occasion when I was on my own in a jazz club – I was about seventeen. There I was trying desperately to read Tolstoy's *War and Peace* but secretly yearning to be part of the crowd. Having a fag and a drink eased the pain a bit but it was a very poor substitute.

I did have one very good friend, Ricky Jarvis, whom I kept in touch with from my previous school. Unlike my cynical friends in Cheltenham, he had a refreshingly outgoing manner and an unsophisticated and natural thirst for knowledge which I found attractive. We were both discovering modern art and literature together. Some of my favourite books of the time were an illustrated dictionary of modern art, the Penguin Book of Contemporary Verse and Robert Musil's novel, *The Man without Qualities*. I also attempted to read James Joyce's *Ulysses,* an unexpurgated copy of which had been given to my father by Uncle Otto. He had bought it when he was a student at the Sorbonne at the famous bookstore run by Sylvia Beach. I remember reading Molly Bloom's speech but not much more! But I did manage his *A Portrait of the Artist as a Young Man* and was inspired to write poetry by reading his collection of poems, *Chamber Music*.

We also discussed politics, which he was far more passionate about than me. I remember going with him to a local labour party meeting and finding it deadly boring. Belonging to CND was as far as I could go in relation to being involved in any kind of political life. (I never made it to Aldermaston. The only time I could go, I had sprained my ankle!)

He often shared with me his intricate experiences of personal relationships. I heard about them or read about them; he lived them. So I led a kind of vicarious existence in that regard. Later in my early twenties when I read Herman Hesse's *Narziss and Goldmann.* I fondly (but reluctantly!) thought of myself as *Narziss*, the Apollonian thinker in contrast to Ricky who was *Goldmann*, the free Dionysian spirit.

One evening we were having one of our intense conversations in his bedsit when one of his book shelves attached to the wall with L brackets came tumbling down, scattering all the books. Rather nervously, I said, 'You must have a poltergeist here', and on the word 'poltergeist' the second shelf fell down. Apparently it is a common phenomenon that psychic disturbances often occur on the occasion of intense emotion during adolescence. This briefly opened a crack in the fabric of the liberal intellectual mindset that we held, like most of our contemporaries, and quickly closed again, not to be opened until I was living in Germany some years later.

Every year Cheltenham had, and still has, a wonderful festival of music which I attended as often as I could, dependent on funds. I saw Vaughan Williams conducting his own 'London Symphony' which I think was his last public appearance. The one that made the most impact on me was a composition by Matyas Seiber, my first acquaintance with modern classical music. I was so inspired that next day I went into my parish church and started composing music on the organ in a sort of atonal way to the psalm, *By the Waters of Babylon*. Unfortunately I was disturbed in my creative endeavours by the church warden who said that the official organist was the only one who was allowed to play it, so that was that. (I didn't compose any more music until decades later when I wrote songs and mood music for plays that I directed).

One of my annoying habits that my friends accused me of then was what they saw as my superior, aloof attitude to other people's viewpoints, whether they were about ideas or opinions about people. I would tend to say, *On the one hand etc... but on the other....* I thought I was being objective, but it could have been that I was just being superficial in my judgement. I just lacked real insight and the courage of my convictions, or rather I didn't have any. This led in the coming years to a kind of impotence of the will. If you see all sides, it is difficult to act and be effective in the world. I came to see it as a dis-ease of the times, diagnosed by Yeats in his poem, *The Second Coming.. 'The best lack all conviction, And the worst are full of passionate intensity, The centre cannot hold...'*. Shakespeare also delineated this condition when he has Hamlet saying, *The native hue of resolution is sicklied o'er with the pale cast of thought.* To find a remedy was another urgent quest I was on, during my time in London five years later.

In 1961 I took my 'A' levels in History, English and French. I cannot remember having applied to a university. I know my eldest brother, David, had somehow secured me a provisional place at Fitzwilliam House, Cambridge, where he and Father graduated. (Bizarrely, Father and my Uncle had bought their M.A.s and received them when David graduated. Apparently in Cambridge in those days, you were eligible for M.A. status so many years after you graduated!). To be admitted, I had to pass their entrance exam which was to take place the following February. Having failed French, I didn't think I had much chance to get in. However the school allowed me to stay another year in the 6th form, to work towards that exam. The only thing I remember about it, apart from the fiendishly difficult questions on *Lear* which I had been studying, was that I didn't know the meaning of the word *obfusc*. Needless to say, I didn't pass. 'The Old Boys Network' had got me that far, but no further. Meanwhile I had applied to other, less rarified places of learning, and it was with great relief when I heard I was offered a provisional place to study philosophy at Southampton University, dependent only upon an interview.

While waiting to go into the interview room, a man went in who looked the part of a philosophy lecturer, with long hair, smoking a pipe. If that's him, I thought, I can display my CND badge. It was a bit different from the normal one in that it had a dotted outline of a cross behind the rune. (Another sign that a residue of

Christianity that I mentioned earlier, still persisted!) Anyway, I hurriedly pinned it on before being called into the interview. One of the first remarks he made was, *Why have you got your CND badge upside down?* Flustered, I muttered something in reply. *This is a great beginning,* I thought. However he soon put me at ease, and we talked about politics, my hobbies such as fencing, and the books I was currently reading. When asked about specifically Western philosophy, I could have mentioned that I was given good marks for a talk I gave on Pascal in a philosophy class at school that the Head had taught. But I completely forgot. However I must have made a favourable impression as a few weeks later in late March, I received a letter of acceptance to the School of Philosophy and Politics. The interviewer, Tony Manser, obviously thought I wouldn't make the grade as a student of pure philosophy. I didn't mind. I had made it! The world suddenly changed. It was the best moment in my life. Now I could leave that school prison which had fettered my spirits for so long. I was a free man, eighteen and a half years old, and the world lay before me. For the next three years I would have the opportunity to explore philosophical ideas with others, not only with fellow philosophy students but with those in other disciplines such as theology and science. I had a rather romantic Platonic view of it all, which was soon confounded when I got to University! But now I was buoyed up in a way I had never been before - everything was possible!

* * * * * * *

3rd Phase. This was preceded by an idyllic interlude. I have noticed while writing this that this was a recurring pattern, - glimpses of a lost Eden before the next phase of descent.

A friend who worked with my brother James, asked me if I would like to accompany him to Greece in the summer, on the back of his motorbike. I said *Yes, I would love to.* I would just have to earn some money to pay for it. So I got a job as a building labourer on a site in Tuffley, Gloucester, near where my daughter is now living, fifty years later. It was hard work. I had to cycle ten miles to get there. I understood for the first time what it must be like for a manual labourer after a hard day's work, to slump into an armchair, pour out a glass of beer, and watch telly, which in my case we didn't have. But I did have the occasional beer. There was a glorious sense of physical tiredness, so different from the mental exertions I had previously experienced. And it was all the more bearable knowing I was just doing this for three months. During this time there was little time for the preparatory reading we were asked to do for the university course. Other more enjoyable aspects of reality were beginning to open up. I had a short, passionate affair with my friend's sister which unfortunately fizzled out when I got caught up with life at University. But it was a significant step into adulthood. (I had a somewhat uncanny experience exactly 50 years later when I found myself in the village where she lived. As I passed by what I remembered as her parents' house, I saw a white-haired lady looking out of the window at me. Of course it couldn't have been her, as I knew she had moved to Wales decades earlier.

But it did look like her. And as I was walking across the common away from her house, someone walking in the opposite direction greeted me. He looked just like my friend, her brother. Memories flooded back and for a moment, it was as if I was caught up in a kind of 'time-vortex'. (That would have made a good short story, I thought).

The day eventually came when we were to set off for Greece. This was going to be an exotic holiday for me. I had only travelled as far east as Austria and had never flown anywhere. (This was still before the age of cheap flights). The bike, a battered old 350cc AJS was loaded up with a tent and pots and pans, a heater and tins of food. I somehow was lodged in between all this on the back seat, which proved to be extremely uncomfortable. I had to get off every two hours to rest my backside. The situation was eased somewhat when I bought a sponge which I tied on. The big end gave way while travelling through France. We were holed up in a remote village for a few days until the local garage managed to obtain a

Resting in Rome

new one. We went over the Alps to Italy, stopped off in Rome and Naples, and got a boat from Brindisi to Igoumenitsa in Northern Greece. I shall never forget the *'rosy-fingered dawn'* that greeted us as we approached land. It was like the beginning of a newly-minted creation. This was the Land of the Gods and Homeric heroes, before the birth of philosophy. Every time we stopped, we were fêted by hordes of children, eager to examine this farting, stuttering machine we were riding on.

We drove down into the Pelopennese and up to Athens, stopping off at Epidauros, the magnificent open air theatre with extraordinary acoustics. How did the Ancient Greeks know what has mostly eluded modern architects?

In the Pelopennese

We camped for a number of days in Athens where we met by chance a group of ex-6th formers of my school which didn't include my two clever friends who had gone with others in an old hearse to Moscow. They both had secured a place at Oxford, and apart from bumping into one of them in London some years later, I never saw them again.

Jo, my travelling companion, was an architectural student, so he was able to help me appreciate the Parthenon. Then came the time to head back home, overland via Jugoslavia, Austria, Germany and Belgium. We had to make sure we filled up with petrol whenever we could in Jugoslavia as petrol stations were few and far between. Also we had to be careful where we pitched our tent as you were only allowed to camp at official sites.

* * * * * * *

I arrived at University bearded and bronzed, filled with excitement and a certain amount of apprehension. In the vast sea of new faces during Freshers week, who was I to latch onto? *Ah, here are some CNDers, I'll go and talk to them.* There were four of us, all doing philosophy – Mike, an exotic-looking, lanky guy who spoke with an upper-class drawl. He had come from Christ's Hospital public school and was very different from other public school acquaintances I had known. He called himself an Anarchist. And then there was Vicky, who tended to drink too much, and the beautiful, light-blond Lorelei. In that first week, we all went down to town and each bought a leather dustman's waistcoat. And I thought I was an individual! Soon we drifted into other circles–Mike left after a year, Vicky became an alcoholic, and the extremely fanciable Lorelei hitched up with a regular guy, and that was that.

For the first two terms my social life was linked with CND. During the Cuba missile crisis we all went on a 24-hour fast and demonstrated outside the American consulate in Southampton, feeling somewhat light-headed! When the crisis was over (I somehow think it was nothing to do with our little demo!) the membership of CND sharply declined, and I was left holding the meagre funds we had accumulated. We had to formally close down the society. Now to pastures anew in the shape of the University Theatre Group. I auditioned for the part of the Chairman of the Critics in the play, *A Resounding Tinkle* by N.F. Simpson, a take-off of the BBC Third programme's art critics panel. I got the part and my performance produced some laughs which was a very satisfying experience. The acting bug was caught. I had done a bit of acting at school but it was not remarked upon. Now I discovered I had a gift.

The philosophical studies in the first year were mildly interesting, but they were not what I fondly imagined – an impassioned quest for the Truth! We didn't converse with those from other disciplines. That happened, if you were lucky, in the pub afterwards. We were asked to write our first essay for Professor MacIver on the subject of Universals. Were nouns like 'beauty', 'chair', 'democracy', 'rabbit', just convenient names or labels for these phenomena or ideas, or were they designating objectively real entities? This was the 'nominalist-realist' debate of the Middle Ages. I wrote mine deliberately not referring to any commentaries, and received as a reward, the remark from the Prof, *Very good...*(and here he paused dramatically)... *for the 12th century!* Well, at least I got there under my own steam! It was the next 800 years of philosophy that I found really difficult to really understand with my *heart* as well as my head, apart from Spinoza.[1]. We only touched on existentialism and phenomenology which had led me to studying philosophy in the first place. Apart from the history of philosophy, the emphasis was on British empiricism with a dash of Continental idealism. Trying to grapple with all the multifarious ideas and their refutations often had the effect of making one's head burst. It was as if you consisted only of a brain with limbs as appendages, with nothing in between. *The holiness of the heart's affections* as Keats puts it, had absolutely no place in this way of approaching philosophy, and still doesn't as far as I am aware[2]. The lectures were delivered well enough, particularly those by Tony Manser, the one who interviewed me originally. His

---

[1] I was in good company as I learned later that he was one of Goethe's favourite philosophers.

[2] See **Endnote 1** for my reflections about what a university could be like in the future.

speciality was Marx and Sartre. I can't say I recall now anything he said, but I do remember his qualities of kindness and patience – an interesting reflection on the importance of what people *are,* rather than what they say. He is one of the key figures in my life to whom I owe a debt of gratitude, not only in taking a risk in accepting me for a place at Southampton, - after all my 'A' level grades were not particularly good – but also for his qualities of character.

* * * * * * *

That summer after my first year, I went with Ricky on his BSA 250cc motor bike to Copenhagen. Driving over the cobbles of some North German towns weakened the spokes of the back wheel, which finally crumpled miles outside our destination. We got a replacement fairly easily and arrived in Copenhagen in a downpour. We managed to erect at the city campsite our little 2-man ex-army tent which proved to be woefully inadequate for keeping out the rain. Having no attached groundsheet, the water gathered around us like a moat. We made friends with an American couple pitched next to us, who introduced us to smoking marihuana. I can't say I experienced much except my heart beat alarmingly faster. That was enough to put me off from trying it ever again!

I can't say I remember much about this holiday, except the beauty of Danish design and Danish girls, the immaculate cleanliness of the streets and the absence of any night life in the towns we passed through.

* * * * * * *

Having discovered the joys (and sometimes the terrors) of acting at the end of my first year, I took a role in *Fairy Tales of New York* by J.P.Donleavy in the Autumn term of my second year, and fell in love with the director, June Mitchell. This fairy tale of Southampton ended happily after the second year! I met her some ten years later after contacting her on seeing her name as the assistant editor in the quality alternative magazine 'Resurgence'. I was invited down to see her and her partner, Satish Kumar, the founder of the magazine. Soon after I was invited to their wedding, a beautiful Indian affair. It was lovely to discover that she, like me, after leaving university had discovered a path of alternative spirituality, which overlapped with mine. When we were together as students we had no interest in, or rather no conception of such an outlook on life.

The next play I was in was a new one called *Dr.Maccabré,* written by Jocelyn Powell, an English lecturer at the University. It was all about a young lover

 called Aquinas (me) losing his faith because his loved one was killed by the Black Death personified by the said doctor (acted by John Nettles[1]). It got into the NUS Drama Finals at Aberystyth in '64 but didn't win. We became good friends for the

---

[1] John years later became famous as *Bergerac* in the television series of the same name; also as DC Tom Barnaby in *Midsomer Murders.* I thought his best acting however, was in his various RSC appearances that I saw.

70

rest of our time at university. In some ways he was similar to my school friend, Ricky. Both came from a working class background. They had a ruggedly individual way of seeing the world – with a combination of emotional and intellectual honesty plus a good dose of humour; all of which I found appealing. In John's case it was particularly in the realm of the mind (he was an astute thinker) while Ricky had a fine novelist's way of expressing the labyrinthine nuances of personal relationships. Again they are people that I owe a debt of gratitude along the path of life, lighting up aspects of human experience which without them would perhaps have remained in the shadows.

The last play I was in, before I decided I had better put some work in for the finals, was Ionescu's, *Jack* which had some fiendishly difficult dialogues to learn. His seemingly absurdist view of life held a great attraction for me then, and twenty or so years later also, when I directed *Exit the King* at the Merlin Theatre. (That production, together with Chekhov's *The Bear* which raised a few laughs from a polite Sheffield audience, brought the house down when it was performed at Botton Village, a Community for those with Special Needs, despite the somewhat metaphysical nature of the play).

While writing this, I looked Ionescu up on the Internet and found the following extract from *The Hermit,* (1973) which in a way explains why he appealed to me particularly at that time of my life.

I thought that it was strange to assume that it was abnormal for anyone to be forever asking questions about the nature of the universe, about what the human condition really was, my condition, what I was doing here, if there was really something to do. It seemed to me on the contrary that it was abnormal for people not to think about it, for them to allow themselves to live, as it were, unconsciously. Perhaps it's because everyone, all the others, are convinced in some unformulated, irrational way that one day everything will be made clear. Perhaps there will be a morning of grace for humanity. Perhaps there will be a morning of grace for me.

It is said that everyone remembers what they were doing when they heard the news of President Kennedy's assassination which was early on in my second year. I was drinking in the union bar when the President of the Students Union came in and made the announcement. Everyone fell silent. It felt like another slippage had occurred in what formerly had been taken for granted—this time of the seemingly secure foundation of Western society. Although I had protested against his policies the previous year, he did seem to embody the idealistic hopes of a new generation. In Britain we still had the old guard, Macmillan and Co. whom we enjoyed seeing being lampooned on *That Was the Week That Was*, (the only TV show I watched while at University, and this was on a small set in the Union). Although our generation did not have to go through the suffering of a world war, nevertheless the fear of nuclear obliteration brought us near to the edge of an existential abyss. Kennedy's death felt we were pushed that much nearer.

In my last year I was asked to audition for a part in *Hamlet* with John as Hamlet, but reluctantly turned it down knowing I had a lot of catching up to do. I had somewhat neglected the politics part of the degree partly because of the boring nature of its factual content and partly because of the unspoken assumptions about human nature that I found in the subsidiary subjects of sociology and economics which one had to do. My philosophical critique of them in an essay I wrote, was met by the response, *That is philosophy, not economics.*

Another reason for not taking part in the play was that anyway I felt I needed a break from theatre life, with all its emotional highs and lows!

The last year went by incredibly quickly, and I was filled with an increasing sense of panic. My head ached with all that we were required to remember, and any original thoughts went out of the window. My only solace was friendship with a few people, music, alcohol, and a feverish spell of gambling, playing pontoon. A group of us ended up owing each other on paper, sums of money we couldn't possibly pay back on our university grants. The whole thing resolved itself when we all disappeared into the ether after leaving University! Another bit of visceral pleasure was going for a spin on my newly acquired second-hand motorbike, the 4-stroke Tiger Cub which was only 200cc but sounded like the roar of a 500.

Apart from my theatre circle, I had become good friends in my first year with Willem Meys, a Dutch M.A. graduate who was doing a thesis on Blake. He was also a painter and he painted a picture of me which attempted to incorporate some of the elements that made up my life – a crucifix, an idealised figure of a woman, a flute, which I had taken up, and the CND rune which in my first year I had not yet abandoned. My abiding memories of Wim was the smell of his cigar, the real coffee which he brewed up, his convivial, phlegmatic temperament, - archetypically Dutch, - and our good-natured banter about life and the universe. Through him I was introduced to Caroline Fawkes who was studying German, a very knowledgeable lady with whom I had a relaxed Platonic relationship. I kept up with both of them after leaving university for some years then inevitably the connections faded out. Wim married a Turkish lady, and suffered the tragedy of having a mentally ill son. He became a lecturer in linguistics and eventually a professor. Caroline became an art history lecturer at St. Martin's School of Art, and then a psychotherapist. Another person who made an impression on me was Jeremy Hooker who had a high sense of mission as a poet. Years later I met him when he was a lecturer in English at Aberystwyth University and already had some volumes of poetry in print. He introduced me to the work of John Cowper Powys whose novels expressed an extraordinary pagan sensibility – unlike anything else I had read. Like June Mitchell, I felt he had to a certain extent travelled in parallel lines to my journey of spiritual discovery.

Apart from these friendships, my other chief solace was music, - both classical and modern jazz, which as I have already mentioned, expressed the spiritual/sensual dichotomy in my nature. A particular favourite LP I cherished in my third year was a Schubert Lieder recital sung by Dietrich Fischer Dieskau, which I had swapped with my brother James for a recording of Britten's *War Requiem.* For some reason, English music never moved me in the way German and Austrian music did, and that is still the case. I was also discovering the strange and exotic sound world of Bartok's six string quartets which for me naturally followed on from Beethoven's last quartets. I loved the way they developed from the more accessible and tuneful First and Second, progressively getting more complex and astringent in the Third and Fourth and finally reaching a higher form of simplicity in the Fifth and Sixth. It could be likened to a journey from the innocence of childhood through the complexities of adulthood to the simplicity of wisdom in old age. True simplicity is not naivety, but complexity refined – a pairing away of inessentials. A similar trajectory is manifest in the development of Shakespeare's plays. His last 'fairy tales' are an octave higher than his earlier fantasies. For example – to continue the musical analogy – the youthful exuberance of *Midsummer Night's Dream* is one end of the scale, *The Tempest* the other, with *Hamlet* in the middle, like the dissonant interval of the augmented fourth (*the Devil's Interval*, as it was called in the Middle Ages). In the C Major scale it is the F sharp, which is exactly in the centre of the scale. I find I am naturally more drawn to the late works of many artists like Beethoven, Bartok, Shakespeare, William Turner and also Mozart –I don't know how many productions of 'The Magic Flute' I have been to, - another fairy tale.

Modern jazz was another passion of mine. I loved the wild freewheeling way a tune was improvised to a point where it was hardly recognisable, then found its way back to the original melodic statement. I suppose also, looking back, it was a kind of dissolute anarchy, an urban despair, which mirrored something that was going on inside me, fuelled by a liberal intake of alcohol. All of this acted as a kind of drug which temporarily relieved a growing sense of meaninglessness. I became friends with Pete Burden, a brilliant fellow philosophy student, who led a jazz quintet with his dazzling saxophone playing. Many a Saturday night was spent listening to his band in a smoky Southampton pub. From the rather tame white modern jazz playing of Gerry Mulligan, and the MJQ that I liked in my late teens, I was now into the wilder, black exponents of the art, such as Charlie Parker, Sonny Rollins, John Coltrane and the cool strains of a Miles Davis. (*Cool* meant something in those days (!) -*detached, unfazed*, the opposite of *sentimental*. Now it is a vague synonym for 'great' – anything you approve of).

Charlie Parker

Although I didn't involve myself with acting in my last year at university, I did make a brief foray into the world of modern dance. I loved the work of Martha Graham whose expressionistic gestures reminded me of Henry Moore; and Merce Cunningham's cooler, sleeker style which I experienced in a live performance at the University. I wrote a review of it for the University Arts magazine, the only piece of writing I had published at the University theatre. I thought I would like to have a go myself so I gathered together a bevy of several female students (no males wanted to join!) and tried to direct them in a dance performance to Milhaud's *La Creation Du Monde*. It was a wonderful mixture of classical music and jazz and somehow had the effect of joining those two worlds of experience within me through the medium of dance. I remember we tried to express in a Grahamish sort of way the beginnings of creation, but I don't think we got further than the First Day, as I didn't really know what I was doing! After some weeks it fizzled out, but it was great fun while it lasted. I retained an interest in dance as I did in all the other arts after leaving university, but didn't have the opportunity to practically involve myself with it again, until years later.

Another brief involvement was with the Anti-Apartheid Movement. I had made friends with a coloured South African activist, a research student who was barred from going home because of his involvement with the A.N.C. His stories of injustice brought home to me what was happening in his country, much more forcibly than reading about it. At that stage many A.N.C activists still believed in non-violent methods, which I learnt something about, at the London School of Non-Violence which he took me to. But there was not much I could do personally to help as the Finals loomed ever nearer.

Near the end of the year, I wrote this poem. I include it here, not because I think it particularly good, but because it gives a bit of a glimpse of the state of mind I was in at the time – a yearning to be at one with Nature and the same time knowing I was ineluctably separate.

Black sleek of a bird
Fluting on a bough outside my window
I leant out and copied his call
One after the other, phon and antiphon
Like a couple of choristers we sang

In those few shrill seconds
I began to feel the weight of wings
And had visions of migrating south
Until I sneezed, that was
And then it winged away
As if to say
He's only a man after all

I left Southampton with a third-class honours degree. Most of my friends got firsts or upper-seconds and some went on to do a Masters or a Dip Ed. Someone said to comfort me that an inglorious Third was far better than a mediocre Second!

I really didn't know what my next steps should be. Half-heartedly, I applied for a liberal studies lecturer's post in a further education college, but was not successful. I also got turned down for a year's voluntary post overseas. It can't have helped attending the interview clutching a book of modern poetry (I think it was Sylvia Plath's), which I had just bought. It must have added to their perception of me as a rather introverted soul who would not be able to take initiative, and I think they were probably right. Thinking back to that time, trying to remember what state of mind I was in, I must have felt rather gloomy and uncertain about my future. All the social support which one naturally had at University was now no more. The idealistic passion for philosophy as a way of seeking meaning in life, which I had had as an adolescent, had evaporated into the thin, cold air of linguistic analysis – analysing the meanings of words – which Anglo-Saxon philosophy was now reduced to, in the 60's, and which we had to study in our third year. Lady Philosophia had become a withered old hag in her last throes, gasping for air. (If I had studied pure philosophy, I might have discovered the late Wittgenstein, who, as a friend many years later pointed out – he had done his doctorate on Wittgenstein and Merleau-Ponty – indicated a possible way forward.) Lack of air – that just about sums up how I felt then. A kind of suffocation of the spirit. (I discovered later, in ancient languages 'air' and 'spirit' was the same word). Looking back I realise I had to go through this particular trial, of everything evaporating into meaninglessness, so that I could create meaning out of my own resources.

I went back home for a few months and got a job in a brewery firm going round pubs tapping barrels. (Unlike now it didn't seem difficult to get a temporary job. Until I found my life's work in my late twenties, I always managed to pay my way). Meanwhile I had asked my Austrian uncle if he could help me find me a post as an English tutor in Austria or Germany. Through an Austrian countess friend of his, he learnt of a German baroness who was looking for someone to teach the younger baronet. This was not exactly what I was expecting! However it sounded a tad more interesting than tapping barrels.

* * * * * * *

4ᵗʰ Phase. Thus it was that I embarked on the next chapter of my life, - to be an English tutor to the young Baron von Ketteler, of the *Schloss Schwarzenraben* (Castle of the Black Ravens) near Lippstadt, Westphalia. I arrived in November 1965, the castle and its moat looming up out of the fog – a somewhat exotic entry into my new life!

(I have to admit that the word 'schloss' does not mean only Gothic or Norman castles in the English sense but huge mansions built in the Baroque era, which this was. But it did have a moat around it!)

I was shown to my room in the servant's wing by the butler, an aged retainer who was the only one they could afford to keep on after the war. I have just learned from Google that Baron von Ketteler disappeared in mysterious circumstances in 1938. He had been the Private Secretary to von Papen and was either assassinated by the Nazis or committed suicide. (Von Papen served as Chancellor of Germany in 1932 and as Vice-Chancellor under Adolf Hitler in 1933–1934. He belonged to the group of close advisers to President Paul von Hindenburg in the late Weimar Republic. It was largely Papen, believing that Hitler could be controlled once he was in the government, who persuaded Hindenburg to appoint Hitler as Chancellor in a cabinet not under Nazi Party domination. However, Papen and his allies were quickly marginalized by Hitler and he left the government after the Night of the Long Knives, during which some of his confidantes were killed by the Nazis).

I was not the only one living in the servants' quarters apart from the butler. The Baroness and her family of three were also living there, due to their straightened circumstances. I was given a warm welcome by the Baroness, a kindly-looking matronly figure and told of my duties which were to give tuition to her 17 year old son every morning. (I realise that this doesn't make sense as he would have to have been much older if his father had died in 1938! But I distinctly remember him as a late adolescent. So perhaps the Baroness was the baron's sister and her husband died later.) The rest of the time I would have free. He turned out to be a somewhat reluctant pupil and was more interested in helping out on the manor farm. So I found myself having more and more time on my own as he skived off to the farm. I spent the time exploring the castle and its magnificent grounds laid out in Baroque style, trying to teach myself German and reading Shakespeare's last plays. There were hundreds of rooms that were closed off. One of them called the ghost room was left open. The Baroness recounted with relish the story of a visiting Catholic priest who was told the story of that room. If anyone moved the picture of a former baroness from off the wall, he or she would be visited by her troubled spirit. She had committed adultery and was either killed by her jealous husband, or committed suicide (I can't remember). The priest, being a good modern liberal fellow, scornfully dismissed the whole story, and to prove that it was just godless superstition, removed it and put it under his bed that night. Something very unpleasant must have happened early in the morning because he left hastily a few hours later. He was due to stay two nights. I naturally was curious to see the said portrait, but needless to say, I left it there on the wall!

On Sunday afternoons I would cycle over to the nearby English army barracks to read the English Sunday papers. On one of those afternoons something occurred which was to fundamentally change my outlook on life. Up to that time I believed there was a beneficent force in the Universe, but not its opposite. Somehow evil was really an absence of goodness, not a reality in its own right. (I remember some years later in a Quaker discussion group, I mildly argued that if existence is to be accorded to something or someone called God, could there not be a being of evil who is also real. It was as if I had uttered an obscenity. The group facilitator quickly changed the subject).

What happened was this: while I was reading the gruesome account of the Moors murders that happened in Lancashire, I had an overpowering sense of the presence of what could be called a cosmic malign force. An abyss opened up in the safe and secure world of enlightened liberal belief that I had been brought up in. A psychologist would no doubt say that it was due to an overheated imagination – a psychic projection of the somewhat anxious state of mind I was in at the time. He would have had a field day about what was to happen next. Feeling physically sick to the stomach, I staggered out of the barracks - by this time it was dark – and was greeted by a dog howling at the full moon which was rising in the late November sky. Although my mind registered the ridiculous Gothic horror cliché of it all, I was nevertheless terrified and pedalled furiously back to the Castle. I tried to exorcise this feeling of utter malignity in the Baroque chapel, whose design was as overwrought as my state of mind!

This was to be the first of a number of experiences that I realised later I had to go through - a series of peelings away of received beliefs and habits of mind that I had either never questioned or had not even been aware of.

It was becoming increasingly evident that my time at the castle could no longer be justified as the young baron simply did not want to learn English, despite the protestations of his mother. So where now? I did not want to return to England, except for Christmas. Just at that moment, the Baroness's two attractive daughters came to stay for the weekend. They told me of the delights of Munster where they were studying, so I thought I would try and find work there for a while. I managed to secure the post of a sergeants' mess assistant (I can't remember how) in the British Army Headquarters in Munster, for which I had to sign the Official Secrets Act. My duties could hardly be called onerous – serving six sergeants with meals, clearing and washing up and generally keeping the barracks shipshape. At night I slept in a dormitory with several squaddies whose ripe language and general conversation was somewhat different to what I had been used to! In the morning we were all woken up by a loud shout and kick on the metal bedstead. This way of life could not have been more in contrast to the previous quiet genteel sojourn in the Castle. I had never felt so socially isolated as I did then. Recalling all this now, it seems as if I had to experience first-hand those aspects of life I was most ignorant of, or against which I had the most prejudice. As a teenager I hated the whole idea of the military and the privileges of the upper classes, and the world of the working class was generally a closed book; a *bildungsroman* I think the Germans call it – a novel which illustrates the life education and character-building of its hero. That's what my life *then* seems to be *now*. Then however, it was experienced as an increasingly meaningless meandering through 'a dark wood' where not only the path was lost but also any sense of a final destination. There was however one gleam of light which managed to penetrate through the dense foliage, and that was my enjoyment of teaching English in the Berlitz School in the evenings. But not even that could dispel the depressive state I was falling into. I did not experience the 'delights' of Munster that the young baronesses had told me of. It seemed to me to be a dreary city with a lot of drunken people staggering around in the middle of the day. It was twenty years since the war had ended, but its after-effects hung like a pall over everything. So the combination of all that, with the bleakness of the weather and the surrounding landscape as well as my state of mind, drove me to the decision to move on. This was around Easter time. I made arrangements to stay with my Uncle in Linz for a while. I gave in my notice to the army and the school and took a train to Austria. [1]

* * * * * * *

5th Phase. Immediately I crossed the border, I noticed a difference. The people seemed friendlier, and the weather brightened up. A feeling of relief surged through my body. My Uncle lived in the same flat that he and my Mother were brought up in. To help him pay the rent which hadn't changed for decades, he took in two lodgers. To augment his small pension, he did some translation work and private tutoring in many different subjects. He was still suffering from alcoholism and his love life still had to be kept secret. Homosexuality was only made legal in 1971 in Austria. He was well looked after by Marie, the same live-in housekeeper who served his parents before the War. Marie had a rather fierce cat called Schnurrli whom one had to treat with great respect.

I managed to find a few tutoring jobs but not really enough to pay my keep. I was about to return to England when my luck changed. Through some new friends I made, I got a job as a window cleaner. The firm was owned by a Pole and my foreman was a Berliner, a hard taskmaster who kept his more relaxed Austrian workers and myself up to the mark. His strictness was in a way justified as we had to clean windows high up on tower blocks using harnesses. I quite enjoyed the

---

[1] I learnt later of the extraordinary courage of one of the sons of Munster, von Galen, its Catholic bishop, who openly condemned Nazi practices throughout their period in office. Because he was so popular, the Nazis didn't dare arrest him.

hard work after all the relative inactivity during my stay in Germany. I would come back from work feeling wonderfully tired and would often spend the evenings with these new friends. During my three-month stay in Linz I visited many of the family friends and relatives I had stayed with after my 'O' levels. They were all very hospitable but I found I had very little in common with them. They were middle-class professionals, well established in life, some with young children. I don't think they could make me out – a graduate who was doing a labouring job. Their focus was on building up their standard of living after all the trauma they or their parents had gone through. They were reluctant to talk about the past. *'Did they know what was going on in Matthausen, a concentration camp near Linz'*, I asked. *'No, we didn't'*, said some. Others gave evasive answers. *'Some of us had suspicions, but remember we lived in a climate of fear. There was an efficient system of informers. Any form of opposition, verbal or otherwise would be severely punished with imprisonment and torture and often death'*.

Listening to this, I felt out of my depth and didn't press them further. Who am I to judge? What would I have done in their place? However this prompted me to continue the inward journey of trying to fathom the mystery of evil that I had begun in Germany, and which I had temporarily put to one side. More particularly, I wanted to find out more about the whole phenomenon of the death camps. I could understand cowardice and fear and feelings of hatred and envy, all those 'deadly sins' that one could be capable of committing oneself, but cold, calculating and conscious acts of evil – these defeated my powers of imagination and understanding. It was several years later that I began to have some sort of inkling of the spiritual reality of it all. [1]

Musing on all my experiences I had, first with living in Germany, and now in Austria, I began to realise how thoroughly English I was, despite my love of their music, literature and philosophy. Looking back, here was another 'skin' or 'costume' that I had to shed. I left England feeling I was really a citizen of the world, a liberal intellectual delusion that is commonly held. I suppose I thought the English way of doing things was really a kind of yardstick of what constitutes civilised behaviour. One was not prone to dangerous philosophical abstractions like the Germans and the French, or unreliable like the Latin peoples or crassly commercial like the Americans. We were a sensible, pragmatic people with a great, self-deprecating sense of humour. Living in a foreign country for some months, it slowly dawned on me that there were other ways of looking at the world or doing things which, assuming one could understand them, were equally valid. It was like discovering that another person whom you thought you knew, had a really different way of experiencing things. Of course all this could be over-simplified. It depends on how close up a portrait you make of a people. My Mother, *a Linzerin,* which is in Upper Austria, could not stand the Viennese, which is in Lower Austria; the Austrians as a whole feel superior to the Germans; the Bavarians dislike the Prussians etc. Some

---

[1] I read later the inspiring story of Franz Jägerstatter, a peasant farmer who lived near Linz. He was executed for his conscientious objection to the War.

wear 'the costume' of their regional or national identity, others believe they have discarded them, but I began to wonder if deep down, beyond the threshold of consciousness, the very structure and usage of the language that they speak, determines the way they think and respond to the world. I was fascinated by the fact that you have to wait until the end of a German sentence before you know what the verb is, and this together with the phenomenon of piling up separate nouns together to make a new composite noun, seemed to me to suggest a valuing of the static nature of the noun over the 'doing' nature of the verb.

(Here is the longest one:-
Donaudampfschiffahrtselektrizitätenhauptbetriebs werkbauunterbeamtengesellschaft. (English: Association for subordinate officials of the head office management of the Danube steamboat electrical services).

Was this a cause or reflection of the fact that concepts are easier to form, hence the abstract, idealistic nature of much of their philosophy? English philosophy on the other hand is more piecemeal, with an emphasis on the perceived particulars, - percepts rather than universal concepts. (Paradoxically, although I felt very English in relation to how I *felt* about things, in my thinking I felt closer to the German mind. Was this due to my half-Austrianness? In which case this would suggest we inherit cultural traits). Another thing intrigued me, and that was the fact that a German, perhaps more than an Austrian, seemed to have no compunction in asking you a direct question, like 'How much do you earn?' whereas an Englishman would think it but not utter it out aloud. We think them rude because they say what they mean. They think we're hypocritical because we don't. I learnt later that there is no gap in between a thought and the word that expresses it, in the German psyche, unlike the English one, where there is. You have to read more between the lines of what an English person says. More is implied than actually spelt out in the spoken word. Perhaps that's why German drama seems less subtle than English drama because everything seems to be made more obvious. The art of theatre as we English understand it, is the art of *showing* a situation rather than explaining it, which leaves the audience free to draw their own conclusions. T.S. Eliot calls this the *objective correlative.*

All this was a beginning of an interest in language and consciousness that I pursued later. Another thing that fascinated me at the time, was whether there was a connection between the shapes of letters, their sounds and how they are made in the mouth. The shape of the letter 'i' (ee) is thin, like the sound it depicts, with the elongated, stretched mouth, whereas 'O' (Oh) needs a roundish shape of the lips, and the sound is more open and expansive like the letter shape. 'K' is made of straight lines that come up against one another. More will is required to create it, with a tension and a release, and the sound is angular, not smooth and rounded; whereas 'B' demands a blowing up of the cheeks, like the bulbous shape of the letter, before the air is expelled. 'm' has a similar shape (on its side) without the straight line as a backbone. It can suggest the rounded nature of the lips when it is uttered, and the continuous, frictionless nature of the sound. I began to wonder if the alphabet arose out of a synaesthetic consciousness that we no longer possess. Again these were questions that I found answers to later on.

Apart from these moments of speculation, and keeping company with my Uncle at 'Sundown' when he had to have his glass of red wine, most of my free time at weekends was spent in the company of those friends I have already mentioned. I met them one evening after a concert at the Bruckner Halle. I was sitting on my own having a drink in the 'gasthaus' nearby. At an adjacent table were two couples in their thirties who cast friendly glances in my direction. They invited me to join them and thus began a warm and lively friendship. They told me later that they thought I must be East German by my rather shabby appearance! Franz played the violin in the Linz orchestra and tended to get more melancholic - in a gentle and delicate sort of way, - the more wine he drank. His wife, Maria, was more merry and sanguine. Hans, a jewellery salesman, was an easy-going, phlegmatic sort of person with highly original views on politics and economics. His wife, Mena, a fiery choleric, completed this quartet of temperaments.[1]. She was unlike any one I had ever met before. I had only read about them in Russian novels! She in fact was a Southern Slav, from Jugoslavia. She had an infectious smile and playful manner, and constantly surprised one in her responses to things – a kind of delightful unpredictability that my young inexperienced and

---

[1] The four psychological types, related to the four elements, which I learnt about later.

'rational' Anglo-Saxon soul simply could not fathom! Her exuberance of spirit pierced through the gloom of my melancholy, and I fell hopelessly and helplessly in love with her. For quite a few years afterwards, she represented a kind of archetypal femininity which no other woman I became involved with, could ever match up to!

She managed lovingly and effortlessly to look after their three small children on Hans' uncertain and usually small income, in a tiny flat that we often all met in. Meals were rustled up from nowhere and wine and conversation on everything under the sun, flowed on until the early hours of the morning. Hans became most animated when he was expounding the ideas of a communal/anarchist economist called Sylvio Gesell. (I learnt years later that they were in some ways similar to those of another unorthodox economic thinker, Rudolf Steiner. They both advocated the idea of 'rusting' or ageing' money).[1]

The weeks passed. Spring was turning into summer. I knew I had to return to England and end this spell in Austria, no matter how vivid and intense the experiences I garnered there. My Uncle's alcoholism was worsening and I felt I couldn't really help him. During one of his episodes, he fell down and broke his leg. While in hospital he was visited by well-meaning friends who brought him cigarettes and his favourite wine which he was allowed to consume on the premises. I was about to leave for England when I received an invitation to tutor a young count in English for a month or so. Well, this was

---

[1] See Steiner's book, *Rethinking Economics*

going up in the world, - not a baron this time, but a count! I couldn't resist the temptation, especially as he lived in a proper mediaeval castle, with courtyards and gardens and a large hunting estate. I had enjoyed my spell of window cleaning and mixing with a friendly bunch of working-class Austrians, but I must admit a change from hard physical labour was inviting. Schloss Gudenus was near the Danube in Lower Austria, surrounded by gentle rolling hills. The young count was

 seventeen and eager to practise his relatively good English, unlike the German baron. He was the eldest of a large family of nine children, presided over by a friendly but rather austere Gräfin von Gudenus. She came to represent for me a calm and disciplined way of conducting life which I had to admire and respect, - completely opposite to Mena who was full of unrestrained, passionate energy. Thoughts of this polarity of soul and spirit became re-awakened a few years later when I was living in London.

The family all sang classical and folk songs and played recorders together. It was all rather captivating. I felt I had stepped back into the Middle Ages. They seemed to own the village which provided the staff to man the castle and its estate. The church was divided in its seating between men and women as well as between the aristocrats and the commoners. If it was in England I probably would have found it unbearable, but here in a foreign country, it all seemed like a fairy tale or a play with an elaborate stage set! They were all courteous and friendly and seemed to live an ordered and unostentatious life. I didn't have much to do with the Graf (the Count). He was busy running the estate. One day he invited me on a deer hunt. I was to blow a decoy deer whistle on top of a hunting tower to attract a buck. I don't remember if it worked, but I do recall being obliged to join the hunting party in their deerstalking hats and *lederhosen*, following a blood trail of a wounded deer. The Count had shot it and failed to kill it outright. That evening there was a feast of venison, which I politely declined! Ever since then I have not partaken of that particular delicacy.

It was the beginning of August. My time at the castle was coming to an end. So was my time abroad.

* * * * * * *

6th Phase. This and the last phase of my 'kali yuga' proved to become the lowest ebb of my life, (again preceded by a prelapsarian interlude). When I returned to England, I was not completely sure what I was to do next. I knew I wanted to live in London and I thought I could try some teaching. I had enjoyed working at the Berlitz School in Germany. I enquired at the teaching agency, Gabbitas and Thring (its offices were as Dickensian as its name!) for any EFL vacancies and was immediately offered a two-week job in Sicily teaching at a 'beach' school. I didn't really want to take it up, as I was now feeling I wanted to get stuck into something more permanent. But the temptation was too great. I had never been to Sicily before and it was well-paid.

Then followed two weeks of paradisal bliss – like a little gift of compensation from the gods for what was to come. The sky and sea was a deep azure blue; it was hot, but not unbearably so; my students were a friendly bunch of young, lively Italians whom I taught on the beach. I hitchhiked round the island with a Jewish girl, a fellow teacher, visiting Palermo and Mount Etna. We didn't have to wait long for lifts and were often invited to our driver's homes. The one experience that has stayed with me was visiting various churches in Palermo, an extraordinary almagam of Norman and Arabic architecture with stunning mosaics that took one's breath away.

So all in all, this Sicilian interlude was a feast of the senses that after just two weeks I found myself becoming sated with. It was as if my daemon was asking me, *So, is this what you really want, a nice uncomplicated sensuous life?* and I was forced to reply, *No, it was good while it lasted, but there's something more worthwhile in life which as yet I still have to discover.*

I came back to London determined to have a go at secondary school teaching. In those days, amazingly enough, you were eligible to teach if you had a degree, even if, like me, it was in a subject or subjects that were not normally taught at school. I went for an interview at the I.L.E.A. (Inner London Education Authority) offices and asked if there was a vacancy for English and Current Affairs. *'Yes, there could be if you would also be prepared to teach lower school maths and French'* 'Well, er, I only have 'O' levels in those subjects'. The interviewer chuckled, *That doesn't matter, as long as you keep a step or two ahead of the class.* I was relegated to a secondary modern school for boys, in Brockley, SE4. On my first day, I was given my time table and shown the various cupboards where I could find the textbooks I would need, and that was about it. Not really having the faintest notion of what and how I should teach, I entered the lion's den with great trepidation and was mercilessly torn apart pretty quickly by a bunch of 14 year-olds. I had made my first fatal mistake – to be nice and friendly and reasonable. I should have remembered my own schooldays. If new teachers didn't immediately assert their authority, they were done for! Eventually above the noise, I found out what they had been doing with the previous teacher – they had had a succession of them – and tried to take it from there. It was an English class and I cannot remember for the life of me what I did with them for the next six weeks. What I do recall was, in a current affairs class I had asked them what they would like to talk about. *'Sex, Sir!'* was the unanimous reply. *'Er, very well'.* So I proceeded to blag my way through. I don't remember what I said, but it kept them in rapt attention for 40 minutes! I had some success with the younger classes, and managed to inspire them to write poetry, some of which was quite outstanding. Maths lessons also seemed to go quite well, but French was a disaster. The projector I was supposed to use didn't work, so I had to resort to good old-fashioned methods of chanting tenses, surreptitiously glancing at a textbook under the desk. My French was never that good.

While I was teaching, particularly in difficult classes, I experience a strange bifurcation of consciousness. One part of me was looking down on the other getting worked up and frustrated, and secretly sympathising with the trouble-makers. Gradually I learnt something of their backgrounds, many of which were dysfunctional – broken homes, inadequate or violent parents. Most of them could be called working-class and a sizeable minority were West Indians. Here for me was another stripping away of another layer of my cultural identity. White and middle-class – my background could not have been more different. And I had had all the solaces of art, nature and religion. These kids had nothing – a bleak and ugly urban environment and reared on a diet of consumerism. The school was not offering anything that could either nourish their inner life or provide them with some practical skills, - just a thin gruel of uninspired second-hand knowledge to be regurgitated up in exams. I felt a rage building up inside me against the whole rotten system, as well as feelings of inadequacy and helplessness that I could do nothing to help. One would have needed to be a social worker, counsellor, psychologist and teacher all rolled into one to help some of those boys. My colleagues did not inspire confidence. There might well have been some good teachers, but going into the staffroom in break time was a depressing experience. In the fug of smoke arose also the 'fumes' of drear conversation about pupils' misbehaviour. I had had enough. I gave in my notice to leave at half-term.

* * * * * * *

What now? I was twenty three and I still did not know what I should and could do with my life. All I knew, or perhaps it would be truer to say, dimly felt, at that time was that it would have to be something I could throw my heart and soul into – a vocation, in other words. Meanwhile I needed to earn something if I was to stay in London. I cannot remember articulating to myself why I wanted to stay there. It must have been a feeling that there was still something to discover there, - a 'spiritual gold' that was eluding me. There was a buzz of energy in the air – it was the mid-sixties – which swirled around me. It was the time of Tolkien mania, Indian gurus and liberated sexuality. I remained a detached observer, - forever the misfit!

Around this time I bumped into my old University mate, John Nettles. He was beginning his professional acting career at the Royal Court, having been noticed by their agent for his Hamlet at the Edinburgh Fringe,-the University production I had declined to take part in. We resumed our friendship and decided to share a flat in Shepherd's Bush, near Goldhawk Road Tube station. I managed to get an EFL teaching post at the Language Tuition Centre in Oxford Street, back to a job I knew I could do well. The pay was £1000 a year which seemed quite reasonable at the time. It adequately covered my basic needs. (My rent was under £4 a week). The only drawback was that I had to teach two evenings a week as well. However compared to the amount of time I had had to spend preparing lessons for my previous job, I felt quite liberated in now having more time to pursue my cultural interests.

The school building was a large cavernous affair with an impressive domed staff room which was deep in the heart of the building. (I learnt years later that masonic rites used to be conducted there before it became a language school). There were twenty or so teachers, many of which wanted to keep to themselves. Gradually I got to know some of them. One of them was a long-haired and shy middle-aged follower of Che Guevara, a large poster of whom plastered the wall in his corner spot; another came and went depending on the pantomime acting roles he could get; another was always in the middle of writing a novel which didn't seem to progress much. The assistant head was a large shambling fellow who tried to keep some order amongst this motley crew of anarchic souls. Gradually it occurred to me that many of them seemed to be in a state of arrested development, apart from me, of course, who for once seemed quite normal! The school was a kind of haven where they could nurse their unfulfilled desires. However there were one or two amongst them whom I got to know better than the others and to whom I owe a great debt of gratitude for essentially changing my life for the better. More about them later.

I loved my teaching. Through drama and mime I managed to get the class enthused and involved. There is nothing like humour, including making a fool of oneself- to get learners to relax and lose their inhibitions about speaking, particularly beginners. It was all Direct Method – only English was allowed in class, which often consisted of many different nationalities. At that time there were more and more Japanese who were quite difficult to get orally involved.

It was hard not to stereotype the different national groupings when you experienced their behaviour en-masse. The Germans were self-confident, the Israelis argumentative, the Latins (French, Italians, Spanish, etc) noisy and undisciplined, the Japanese, studious, etc

etc. I wonder how a group of English students would be perceived in a foreign language class!). I taught at all levels up to the equivalent of A level, which meant learning all about the structure of the English language which was only lightly covered at my Grammar school. In my last year at the Language Tuition Centre, a language laboratory was installed, incorporating the latest recording devices. It was an effective tool for drilling conversational phrases but no substitute for real live interaction between teacher and students.

I came to life in my work. It was after all a kind of theatre, but off-stage it was very different. I began to feel more and more an aching kind of loneliness which acted like a corrosive acid at the pit of my stomach. Everyone else, (apart from my fellow teachers, which I suppose was some kind of perverse comfort) *seemed* normal and stable. They had girlfriends or boyfriends or in the case of my three brothers, had wives and children. They had found their life work and didn't anguish over existentialist questions about life. What was wrong with me? Was I incapable of love? I didn't have a regular girlfriend – just short term relationships. I was madly in love with a Portuguese girl (not one of my students) but it was unrequited. She reminded me of Mena, so of course it was bound to fail! In any new social situation, outside work, I relied more and more on alcohol to get over my debilitating shyness. With a few drinks inside me, then of course I felt relaxed and confident. Again it was a kind of acting   another personality. *Where was the real me?* I began to ask myself more and more. On top of that, I began to develop a phobia for being looked at by strangers in public spaces, like on the tube or in pubs. I felt so ashamed of this condition that I could not confide in anyone that I had this experience. After all, I was not a teenager anymore. There was one time that I did tell someone when I was a little drunk, and he admitted to the same condition, which was comforting to know I was not alone.

I sought spiritual help for my condition from a monk who was suggested to me by my brother, who was in the same Order. But being exhorted to turn to Christ for help, was of no use. So I turned to psychology and enrolled on an evening course. This proved to be even more irrelevant, with paltry verifications of the theory of behaviourism. One experiment we did was to measure the number of spontaneous remarks your speaking partner made if (a), you showed interest in what he was saying, and looked at him directly, comparing it with (b), when you looked away. Lo and behold, everybody discovered (a) yielded more spontaneous remarks!

Then I came across the book, *The Divided Self* by R. H. Laing. This was a revelation. Here was someone talking my language – an existential phenomenological study of the self - but not only speaking the same language but diagnosing my malaise. Here was

described the symptoms of our modern condition of being regarded as a thing, not as a person. That was exactly how I felt – as an object, not as a subject, and it made me think of how I could be treating others.

I did not find a 'remedy' in his book, but at least my condition was recognised, which in itself was a wonderful relief. It also re-awakened my philosophical quest for wholeness. I just could not accept that the fractured nature of scientific knowledge, - no matter how successful it was in relation to the world of matter and machine, - was capable of properly understanding the nature of our human experience. Gradually, the question began to formulate itself, '*Can there be a psychology that acknowledges the spiritual as well as the mental (as in psychoanalysis) and the physical (as in behaviourism) sides to our nature?* It was to be another year or so before I began to get something of an inkling of an answer.

The present state of religious understanding that I was acquainted with then, was also inadequate for both my spiritual and social life. I reasoned, *If Christianity is true, then it must apply to every aspect of life.* There must be a radical re-appraisal of *everything* – how we know and perceive things, how we order our social and economic life, how we express ourselves artistically. The Incarnation was such an extraordinary claim – it was either complete nonsense, or a nice, comforting story that we assent to on a Sunday and deny practically the rest of the week, *or* it would mean we would have to re-instate the spiritual reality of the human being as the centre of every kind of intellectual, social and personal endeavour, rather than it being pushed to the margins of life. If the Divine became human, then we cannot be reduced to an economic unit, a biological organism, a complex machine. In this light, we need a new way of knowing that encompasses the whole of reality. Where was I to find such an understanding within a Christian framework? Despite everything, I still had a residue, - a *feeling* of the reality of Christ, - even though I could not integrate it into the rest of my experience. I did not attend church or associate with Christians. The middle-of-the-road Anglicanism of my father and brother no longer spoke to my condition, but I appreciated its tolerant spirit; the evangelical ethos, whose adherents were often genuinely friendly, I nevertheless found quite alien with its emphasis on a narrow kind of belief, rather than thinking for oneself. That left the liberal demythologised form of Christianity that I became attracted to in my late teens. By now I found it less and less satisfactory because of its uncritical acceptance of the secular, reductionist way of thinking in all other spheres of life, (a dualistic division between belief and knowledge). In order to accommodate itself to what it thought as modern science, it had ditched all the old insights of theology, - including notions of evil that for me by then was a reality, - thus throwing out the baby with the bathwater. Because of its eagerness to be rational, the mystical side was abandoned. Depth was sacrificed to breadth. And the irony is that they were in danger of being left stranded as science itself was moving on, at least in the field of theoretical physics where the 19th century notions of matter were dissolving into fields of consciousness. *So this question of where I could find a 'universal' Christianity which had both depth and breadth, was left hanging in the air.* Outwardly, I managed to do my job well, but inwardly I was falling apart. The only thing that kept me together was the kind of impassioned thinking that was swirling around in my mind, and the friendship of one or two people. I didn't see much of John, who was acting in the evenings, but whenever we met, some of the old philosophic fire began to flare up. After about six months, he left, - I think to move in with his girlfriend, and I fell into a sort of will-less state where I felt a complete lack of self-motivation to do anything. I suppose that could be described as the beginning of clinical depression. I knew I would have to find another tenant to share the rent, or move out and find a bedsitter. But I did nothing for weeks. Then something happened which was like a kind of miracle. I was beginning to take an interest in the music of Anton Webern[1], an atonal composer. I was sufficiently motivated in this instance to pursue this new pleasure, so I borrowed from Hammersmith Library the record set of his Complete Works. (He wrote very short pieces!). I

Webern in his beloved Alps

don't know what it was, whether it was the pure, crystalline nature of his music and the sheer, strange beauty of his songs, but it had a kind of cathartic effect. I felt cleansed and renewed. Something mysterious and exciting beckoned me on the horizon. Whatever it was, I knew I had to go and explore it. Hope was reborn. The next day after listening to it, I went out to look for somewhere else to live. I don't think I had ever had an aesthetic experience like that before, which so directly activated my will. (James once described to me a similar experience of Art dramatically

---

[1] Years later, I read in his little book, *The Path to the New Music*, that he was inspired by Goethe's understanding of Art and Nature. A similar magical feeling of discovering a kindred spirit arose a few years ago when I heard a cello piece on the radio which I loved. Here was a new kind of music that I was looking for. The composer was someone I had not heard of before –Sofia Gubaidulina. I discovered later that she was influenced by Webern, and also by Anthroposophy.

affecting Life, when he and Christl, his wife, had gone to a performance of Wesker's *Roots*, and it inspired them to get out of the rut they were in. They decided to go to Austria for a holiday, although they really couldn't afford it. They had been trying to have a child for a long time but without success. But on that holiday, their daughter, Maria, was conceived. Another example was the cathartic effect, in the classic Aristotelian sense, of a play I directed, Yeats' *Resurrection,* on someone, who told me years later that he felt a great burden had been lifted from him after seeing it).

* * * * * * *

7th Phase. I was now living in a bedsitter in *Goldhurst Terrace*, Swiss Cottage, sharing the kitchen with two others. The rent was £4 a week, a reasonable amount for a large, light and airy room, unlike the small and gloomy basement flat near *Goldhawk Road*. At work, I was beginning to form a close friendship with Robin, a fellow teacher, whose desk was next to mine in the staffroom. His whole manner intrigued me. A few years older than me, he was far more knowledgeable in most things. He had had a good degree in philosophy from London University. What was he doing here, which was in a way a dead-end job? His recent life-story gradually emerged. He had been living with his girlfriend in Portugal, writing a novel. Then he became involved in black magic and a spell was cast on him. I listened to all this with mounting incredulity. Surely he was spinning me a yarn? Up till then, I was only acquainted with the occult as it was presented in the tabloids, apart from the few 'supernatural' experiences I have already mentioned. I was simply ignorant of the anthropological evidence for the existence of magical practices in all parts of the world. My religious and intellectual education had not mentioned anything about that. Listening to Robin calmly and cogently describe his own condition as well as this whole strange new world, had the effect of disturbing another part of the foundations of my conventional religious and rationalist worldview. Nothing seemed secure anymore. It was like what a Sufi friend said to me a few years later when he asked me to contemplate the following sequence of thoughts: *'I know that I know things. I also know that I don't know things. But really experience the effect of saying, 'I don't know what it is I don't know'.* A huge abyss opens up.

Robin never fully explained how it all happened. But he did say there is a difference between black and white magic. The former is used to serve your own egoistic ends; the latter is only possible if your motives are pure. He then told me about the whole magical, or esoteric tradition of the West, such as Rosicrucianism, alchemy and astrology, as well as the Hermetic sciences which re-emerged in the Renaissance. He did not tell me then, but I learned subsequently that many of the revered cultural figures of the past were influenced by occultism[1], including Albertus Magnus, the teacher of St. Thomas Aquinas, and Isaac Newton, who spent far more time on his alchemical studies than he did on what became the foundation of modern science. These were white magical systems, which sometimes were misused

---

[1] The word *occult* simply means *hidden* – not revealed to the physical senses. Another word that is used to mean the same thing is *esoteric.*

and corrupted, like for example the alchemists who, instead of searching for the spiritual gold of a higher form of consciousness, were prompted by greed and were intent on making physical gold. And it was these decadent practices which became the butt of satire and ridicule, and since the Age of the Enlightenment in the 18th Century, any self-respecting intellectual couldn't possibly take these things seriously. As a result of which, both the religious and academic establishments have effectively put their own kind of spell on us and convinced us that these phenomena either don't exist or they are not worth taking seriously. (An exception is the work of the academic historian, Frances Yates in her studies of Rosicrucianism).

Listening to Robin describing this whole new world to me as I was then, I found, as I have already said, my credulity strained to the limit. But I had to take him seriously. He was able to engage in perfectly reasonable discussions about literature – we had read many of the same books, - philosophy and life generally. I made a mental note that one day I would have to make my own studies of esotericism. For the present I was more concerned about his mental condition, for there was something wrong. If I hadn't been told that he was literally under a spell, I would have said the same but meaning it in a metaphorical sense. Like many of the other teachers, he seemed to have come to a kind of emotional and spiritual standstill. By gaining his confidence he gradually came out with what happened to him as a result of this 'bewitchment'. His will became crippled. His energy and zest for love and life deserted him, as a result of which his girlfriend left him, he stopped writing and returned to England, an empty shell. He came to live with his mother in Brighton and was now commuting each day up to London. He sought both psycho-analytical and psychiatric help and neither treatments worked. (For these doctors and therapists, of course, his beliefs were delusions). This made me recall the question I had been living with. *Is there something beyond these two kinds of understandings of the human being which can bring about healing?* I noticed as time went on that he was becoming more alive and expansive. Was there something in our relationship which was beginning to have a healing effect? Now the question, *'Could there be a psychology based on Love?'* shone out like the sun through clouds. In other words, *'Can psychology have a spiritual dimension?'*

That was yet another question for which I had to await an answer. If I am to try now and give a picture of what my mental state was like then, it would be something like this: *I was out of my depths in a huge dark ocean, in a constant state of near-drowning. The only thing that buoyed me up was the sight of colourful fish flashing by (those were my classroom experiences) and the occasional rays of light piercing the gloom. (Those were the various thoughts and questions I was articulating to myself).*

Around this time, an image from my time abroad rose to consciousness. And this was my experience of Evil. I came across a book in a London second-hand bookshop about the death camps of Treblinka, and it described how everything was carefully and consciously planned to the last detail – a cold and deliberate perpetration of evil. I can still vividly recall the feelings I had on reading it and wanting to shout out aloud, *How on earth can people go on in life in the same old way, as if this had not happened? Surely everything has to change. How we understand and conduct our life cannot remain the same. All present-day art, all philosophy, all our superficial religious notions, have to bow down their heads in silence.*

(Years later, I came across the extraordinarily symbolic story of Goethe's Oak when I visited Weimar where he lived, - described as a Northern School of Athens of the 18th and 19th centuries, expressing the best of the German spirit. Nearby is the site of the concentration camp of Buchenwald which I also visited. There can still be seen the stump of the oak tree where Goethe composed some of his love poetry. Its old gnarled remains had been left standing by the Nazis until an American bomb fell on it and burned it to the ground.)

Another dream image arose out of my time abroad. This was of the two women in Austria, but now rising to consciousness as living archetypes, the Apollonian and Dionysian poles of existence, which I have already mentioned. But now I began to experience them as being taken to extremes, - distortions that can have a baleful influence upon life. The impulse for form and order, if exaggerated, leads to a kind of sterility and a belittlement of the heart; the other, if not checked, brings about passionate abandonment and loss of self. I was beginning to be strongly aware of these two forces pulling me (and other people) into opposite directions, and all sorts of different phenomena, - social, political, artistic, religious, - were manifestations of the same energies, making them dangerously one-sided and unbalanced.

This was the beginning of another exciting set of discoveries, which I began to write down over a period of weeks.

These two destabilising forces as I characterised them then, I felt as being real and not just as metaphors. And their operation in the world helps to build a ladder down into deeper and darker realities. After all, the fanatical enthusiasm of a fascist crowd was the manifestation of the one, while the bureaucracy that efficiently ran the whole machine, was an expression of the other. In this instance they were working together.

In milder and less dramatic ways, the, let me call it, *Yang* force (which I learned later from the Daoist philosophy), I could see all around me, and within me.

If not moderated, it leads to soullessness, cynicism and despair. It is the head dominating our feelings, the cool intellect pouring scorn on the effusions of the heart. It manifests outwardly as the 60's brutalist architecture that was all around me in London; the reductionist nature of our science (behaviourism in psychology) and the atomistic nature of urban society, which is its mirror image. Lonely souls colliding in a meaningless void. It is the purely cerebral and specialised education I suffered from, at school and university, which gives us more knowledge about less and less. It is the fall from wisdom to knowledge and now in our time to information. It is the clever manipulations of advertising, factory farming, a spoof democracy of voting every five years, and the alienation of labour as Marx called it. It knows the price of everything and the value of nothing. It is the electronic outpourings of some contemporary music, the rationalistic tendencies in modern theology. It is a colourless world of straight lines, machines and the banishment of Nature.

Recently I have come across something that the Dalai Lama said, (apart from the line about computers, which weren't around then for personal use), which characterises much of what I felt then as that *'yang'* or *'masculine'* force, as I called it.

We have bigger houses but smaller families.
More conveniences, but less time.
We have degrees, but less sense;
More knowledge, but less judgement.
We've been all the way to the Moon and back,
But we have trouble crossing the street
To meet the new neighbours.
We have built more computers to hold more information,
To produce more copies than ever,
But we have less communication.
We have become long on quantity, but short on quality.
These are times of fast foods but slow digestion.
Tall man but short character.
Steep profits but shallow relationships.
It is a time when there is much in the window, but nothing in the room.

Conventional religious thinking presents a picture of good and evil, whether in a metaphorical or literal sense as opposites, like black and white. What I was now realising is that there are *two* kinds of negative energies which destabilise the soul and society. (At that time I could not yet relate this discovery to the existence of a deeper power of Negation, an experience of which I had had in Germany).

In reaction to the one-sided emphasis on the intellect, on quantity rather than quality, as characterised above, many of my contemporaries (including myself), were seeking solace in a variety of ways, the essential effect of which was to feel liberated from the straightjacket of reason and the isolation of the soul, into a feeling of merging into a greater whole. This took on different forms, qualitatively different from each other, but nevertheless all sharing a common trait of over-valuing sensation and feeling against thinking. I suppose it was like the Romantic reaction to the Enlightenment in the 19th Century. I was reading Eric Fromm, a psychologist, at the time and he deftly characterised this *'Yin'* or *'feminine'* force in the field of personal relationships and also in politics and society. In *The Art of Loving,* he says we incline to, or veer between what he calls the 'masochistic' tendency where we lose our identity in the other-this is the illusion of romantic love, – and the 'sadistic' tendency, which is often the reaction of disillusionment, of not showing your feelings and making the other into an object, to be coolly observed.

In this state you are invulnerable to suffering. Here he delineates the imbalance I was becoming aware of at the  time. In his book, *The Fear of Freedom* he describes the Nazi and fascist phenomena as being a reversion to an earlier societal form of tribalism where the individual is submerged in the mass, manipulated by a leader. For me he was describing the same Yin force. Nationalism (not patriotism, which is a justified love of one's country) is erotic and romantic love writ large – a kind of narcissistic egotism.

Other illusory states of losing oneself were the effects of alcohol (which I knew first-hand) and the taking of drugs, which I had experienced others taking. Experimenting with LSD was quite common at the time. Many people were influenced by Aldous Huxley's book, *The Doors of Perception* written in the 50's, which recounts his experiences with mescaline. He compared his ecstatic visionary sensations to the various mystical states attained by arduous religious training. I could see why people were attracted to this way of escaping from the drear and colourless life of the intellect, into a heightened experience of reality where all the senses are vividly engaged. After all, was it not used in some ancient spiritual practices, but without the tedious moralising and dogmas of conventional religion? However I was not convinced. A chemical shortcut to spiritual bliss without real inner work seemed a dangerous illusion. There were many 'bad trips' one heard of, and cases of mental illness.

One day, I got talking to some young people who were members of the Hare Krishna movement. I often heard them chanting in Oxford Street, outside my classroom window. I wanted to find out what motivated them. Some of them said they had been on drugs but were now free through their devotion to Krishna. Intoning a mantram brought about an ecstatic state of consciousness in a safe way. They radiated happiness but I could not help feeling that their real being was not present when we were talking together. 'Blissed out' was how I expressed it to myself. However, I respected their sincerity and saw that they were better for not being dependent on drugs anymore. Also I was aware that Hinduism, of which they were a modern Western variant, was a profound religion. Who was I to judge? I just knew it was not a path for me.

I was invited to a 'satsang' by another Hindu group, a devotional meeting where their guru would give them instruction. I remember he talked about Christ (did he think I was a follower?). He said Jesus didn't really die on the cross. Somehow his body had been substituted by another. He really went to India and continued his mission there. The next day, I jotted down the thought, 'Jesus didn't die. Was a god only'. I put that in my Yin column. In the other column I wrote, Jesus as human being only. Resurrection just a metaphor. (One of my favourite one-act plays, The Resurrection by W.B.Yeats, powerfully dramatizes these polar opposite conceptions of Christ and offers a third possibility).

Another experience I had at the time was encountering scientology, through a girl I knew who was beginning to get involved with it. Here I was in no doubt that this was a dangerous cult, combining pseudo-religious practices with philosophical and occult gobbledegook. It lured people in with promises of self-realisation, for which they had to pay increasing amounts of money.

For me it was becoming increasingly clear that any religious or spiritual path could not have leaders, whether priests or gurus, who would tell you what to think and do. Freedom and clarity of thought is paramount. At the same time, it would also have to be both mystical and practical, as I have said earlier, and would have to include somehow the reality of Christ[1]. Such a path I had not yet found. I continued to characterise various other phenomena as being expressions of these two forces and in some cases, tried to see if there could be 'a third way'. Although I realised they were crude generalisations and a simplistic series of opposites, I nevertheless felt they were indicating something archetypally real lying behind them. I hadn't systematically worked it all out, but there was a growing sense I was onto something.

Yearning for the past v. rushing prematurely into the future; Man as angel v. Man as animal or machine; mystical feeling v. the rational intellect; Matter is Maya (illusion) v. Spirit is Maya; popular culture v. 'high brow'; rococo and romantic styles like Gaudi v. classical and functionalist architecture; (Could there be a psychological and spiritual kind of functionalism – a built environment that serves our essentially human needs and not just our practical ones? A building that most excited me then was Corbusier's Chapel at Ronchamp, a beautifully flowing but balanced sculptural shape). Communal living in the country v individualistic living in the city; (Can there be communal ways of urban living which still allow

---

[1] I felt uncomfortable in speaking about God or Christ openly. It seemed to me that many religious believers too readily assume a cosy, personal relationship to Him, whereas they could well be personifying a rather subjective notion of what they *imagine* to be their deity. The second commandant of Moses is not often obeyed, 'Thou shalt not take the name of the Lord thy God in vain'. However I felt the word 'Christ' did convey to me some sort of reality to me, no matter how hazy, so I am writing it here because that's how I named that reality at the time.

individual privacy?). Right v left politics; art and religion v. science. (The 17th century philosopher Locke said that only what can be weighed, measured and counted, is objectively real; art and religion are merely subjective). *Giving free reign to our instincts v. puritanical morality; symbolic versus naturalistic art (painting, drama etc). (Could there be a form of 'spiritual realism'?)* I even brought it down to the contrast between vowels and consonants and between curves and straight lines! *The subjective expressionism of much modern dance versus the highly worked out system of classical ballet. (*I came up with the idea of a future form of dance which would express the sounds of language, - the shapes that vowels and consonants make, in the way I had been thinking about earlier when I was in Austria. It would combine the 'objective' nature of language with the 'subjective' content that was being expressed. It remained an idea as I didn't have a group of dancers to try it out with!).

I was of course not saying these various phenomena were wrong in themselves, but the 'power' or 'energy' that they were expressions of, if one-sidedly dominating our personality and our culture, could lead to a diminution of our humanity. Science and rationality are necessary for our human development; any artistic expression can be justified; and the various forms of religious life still serve a purpose for many people. It's just that I felt they were all in need of further development. It was as if their trajectories had come to a standstill. And that sense of being 'stuck', an immobility of spirit, was just as true regarding my own inner life.

Many years later I was able to come up with an image which expresses these polar opposite forces. We are tight rope walkers, continually readjusting our balance as we move forward. We are always in danger of falling to the earth on our left, (the harness doesn't work) or if we fall to our right, we are left dangling in the air (in this case the harness does work). In both cases we can't move forward. However, it is actually the dynamic afforded by these opposing forces which enables us to do so.

During my three years in London, as much as my modest salary allowed, I went to various cultural events – films, plays, concerts and exhibitions. I loved the lyricism of French films, the gritty realism of English ones and the satirical Italian ones. But the ones that attracted and intrigued me most were some of the Czech ones, particularly *Closely Observed Trains* which seemed to combine all those qualities. It was the Slavic enigma again! I was still nourished by classical music and early modern art. As for theatre, I appreciated the dramatic skills employed in depicting the anguish, absurdity and despair of contemporary life, by Osborne, Pinter, Albee and others, but came away from the performance feeling vaguely unsatisfied. Yes, there was a kind of honesty, but also a complete lack of a sense of the transcendent, which I was yearning for. The only playwright I felt was near to what I was looking for, was Samuel Beckett. There was a kind of austere beauty (like Webern) that appealed to me at the time. His plays were just as 'honest' as other modern plays, if not more so. However because their uncompromising bleakness and stripped-down metaphors of the human condition were expressed poetically, they were strangely transcended. It was as if he was the only one courageous enough to stare into the abyss –a kind of secular *via negative.* Not this, not that.

We *are* talking heads. We *do* live will-less, fixed lives. My question was, *What can come after Beckett?*

Some 'avant-garde' art I found philosophically interesting, like Marcel Duchamp's creations, such as the public urinal - a manmade object taken out of its usual context. It made you see it in a new light, - an abstract form. Perhaps in the future we will be able to transform all our mundane reality into an aesthetic experience. However this was a *mental* response to his art - interesting - but it didn't engage my whole sensibility. I was looking for an art that was both visceral and spiritual. The meditations on intense colours of some of the abstract expressionists I suppose, came near to it.

In relation to contemporary music I found I was becoming increasingly alienated by its harsh atonal complexities, and that applied equally to the 'free' jazz of Ornette Coleman, Albert Ayler and others. I was intrigued by the work of John Cage whose work was influenced by oriental mystical ideas, including the chance elements in the *I Ching*. His ultimate piece for me was the piano composition, *4'33"*, which entailed the performer not playing the piano for 4 minutes 33 seconds. This silence was intended by Cage to enable the audience to listen to the sounds around them in the environment, - an aural equivalent to Duchamp's visual experiment. *After that, what next?* I made a next step when I attended a 'workshop/performance' by his English follower, Cornelius Cardew. I arrived late, so I didn't hear his introduction, so what greeted me on entering the hall was 'the audience' 'performing' an incomprehensible series of silent movements, with people climbing on tables and getting off again, others ripping up newspapers, others lying down. Had I come into a madhouse? On the principle of, *'If you can't beat 'em, join 'em'*, I entered into the spirit of things, and started miming a talk, with exaggerated facial and hand gestures. A man who was 'listening' to it, got up from the floor, came up to me and silently handed me a note upon which was written, *'The best thing yet!'* (Thinking about it now, it might have been something to do with the theme of chance but who knows). I learnt later that Beckett had written two plays, *Act Without Words, I and II* which was a series of mimes. Obviously I had tuned into the Zeitgeist!

My heart was yearning for beauty and significance in all the arts. By beauty I didn't mean an easily-won sentiment of well-being. There needed to be a certain amount of ugliness or discord (which is after all a part of the human condition), in contrast to any hint of a higher order of meaning. One couldn't go back to earlier models. *Where then? Is that all that is left – a vatic silence before the abyss?*

All these questions were left hanging in the air.

Around this time, towards the end of my second year in London, I was sustained, in an otherwise bleak social existence, by reading some of Thomas Mann's novels, particularly *Dr Faustus* and *The Magic Mountain*. Here I found a kindred spirit, someone who was depicting all the major questions I was wrestling with. He  provided no answers. His position was the ironist, *the incognito moralist*, as I think he called it. Nevertheless his art validated my life at the time and kept me sane. In both novels, various characters embody in different ways the Dionysian and Apollonian forces at work in Germany and in modern Western society generally. I could identify with the central character, Hans Castorp, in *The Magic Mountain,* who comes to visit a sick friend in a sanatorium, and has to stay there because he has become ill himself. There he is torn between conflicting influences, and manages to leave after seven years, only to become a soldier in the First World War. The author sees him as a kind of questing knight, the pure fool Parsifal, in search of the meaning and purpose in life, - the Grail, - in other words. I was beginning to regard the rotunda staffroom at the school as a kind of sanatorium where people were condemned to stay for the rest of their lives! In *Dr Faustus,* the rise and fall of Nazism is symbolised by the account of the central character's life, whose pact with the devil parallels Germany's selling its soul to Hitler.

That summer of 1968, I went for a holiday to Austria, and called on my old friends. There I also joined up with a party of English people led by my eldest brother, Father Bernard, as he was known in his monastery. It included my Mother and Olga, my sister, and a family whose youngest daughter, Judith, was later to become my wife. Apart from briefly seeing each other again a month or so later in London, it was not until twelve years later that we met again and this time fell in love and got married.

Going back to work after the holidays, life continued on in much the same way. I was still pre-occupied with the question of how to balance or rather transcend those opposing energies I have delineated above. I felt frustrated at not being able to convey to anybody, including even Robin, the fact that I passionately *experienced them as realities,* and were not merely intellectual speculations. Then a new line of thinking opened up which moved things on considerably. A number of things rapidly flowed together – my learning from Robin about ancient knowledge and reading some anthropology, Thomas Mann's novels and particularly Erich Fromm's *The Fear of Freedom.* Luminous thoughts poured into my mind.

The Yin/Dionysian/feminine powers were legitimate psychic and spiritual forces of the ancient past. But humanity eventually had to evolve to the opposite state of consciousness, the one we have now, in order to acquire self-awareness and freedom of thought. That is, we had to lose our feeling of unity with the Divine, with Nature and each other in order to direct our lives from within outwards. The age of the pharaoh, the guru, the priest, is over. But, and it is a big 'but', in the process we have become lonely, alienated creatures who no longer have access to the ancient wisdom to guide our lives. We are confused and directionless. If this state of affairs continues, we are in danger of not only destroying Nature but also our own souls. I then asked myself, **Is there a way of regaining what we once had lost, - not going back to an illusory past,- but now retaining the ability to think independently and freely uniting it with our powers of feeling and imagination, - a reunion of the heart and mind? And a reconnecting with the whole, without losing our sense of self.**

I pictured this evolutionary process as a figure **U**, or rather as a parabola,[1] with a descent down the left side, and a possible re-ascent up the right side.

I felt elated. Although I was left with yet another question, I seemed to be getting closer to solving what could be described as a great spiritual and psychological riddle.

I was in a strange state of soul. I was buoyed up with these thoughts but on the other hand I was becoming more despondent and gloomy about my future. I loved my teaching, but I couldn't imagine doing it for the rest of my life, particularly at this school where a kind of 'spell' had been cast on its staff. I was wanting a vocation where I could do some good in the world and to which I could commit myself heart and soul. The nearest thing to that that I could think of was to become a social worker. (I blush now to think how naïve I was!). Accordingly, I thought I would do some voluntary work in the community to experience what it was like. Just at that point, Ricky, my old school friend, got in touch with me. He was now living in London with his wife. In his spare time he was active in a community project in Notting Hill in which he invited me to take part. From that brief experience and also from a spell in Toynbee Hall in the East End, I learnt two things,-about myself and others. My wish to 'do good' was a sentimental one. I didn't feel strong enough in myself to really help others. And I noticed that many of my co-workers were

---

[1] Later, I became intrigued by the thought that the mathematical figure of the parabola shares the same Greek root as the word 'parable'. A parabola is a figure whose ends join at infinity, while a parable is an earthly story with a heavenly meaning.

as much filled with the 'sins of Old Adam' –pride, envy, fear etc as anyone else who was not purporting to 'help others'. Yet another naïve expectation! If I had known Gandhi's quote then, I would have said, _Be the change you want to see in the world._

The questions I had seven years previously as an adolescent, came flooding back with redoubled force – but re-expressed in a slightly different way. However the soul dynamics were the same. I experienced myself as being pulled in three different directions, - by my thoughts, my emotions and my actions. I had the conscious intention to do or be good but was prevented by unbidden feelings of anxiety and inadequacy from carrying it out. Or I was subject to powerful emotions of sympathy but they found no outlet in practical action, or if they did, they were often proved to be unwise. That is, I hadn't really thought clearly enough about the possible consequences. The question I asked was, _'How can I integrate these powers so they can work together'?_ It was really the question, which never left me, _'How can I love more fully'._ I knew love was the most important thing in life, but what is it that prevents one from carrying it out, both from within oneself and in the society one was living in? I could not find any practical help in any of the psychological or spiritual literature I was reading. Then something happened which was to change (among other 'miracles') the course of my life...There was another person in the staffroom that I got to know a little. He was one of those people who spoke little, but you felt when he did speak, there was a wealth of experience behind his words which commanded respect. He also had an impish sense of humour which greatly attracted me. I can't recall now much that we talked about, but I do remember him urging me to read *The Little Prince* by St. Exupéry[1]. (Seven years later, I made it into a play which I directed in Sheffield). Apart from that gift to me, I shall always be indebted to him for inviting me to

accompany him to a talk on Buddha's Eightfold Path given by the Venerable Sangharakshita[2] in Notting Hill. I was transfixed. Waves of relief flooded my body. Here was what I was looking for – a practical way of achieving harmony in the soul. *Right Understanding, Right Intention, Right Speech, Right Livelihood, Right Effort, Right Mindfulness,* and *Right Concentration.* They were not just enumerated as a list of virtues, but there were exercises you could practice which could help you achieve them. At the end of the talk, there was a little Buddhist ceremony that was enacted. I was intrigued but I couldn't really relate to it. I remember very clearly at that point asking myself, *Could there be a Christian form of the Eightfold Path?*

Another powerful experience I had round about that time was I suppose the nearest to being a mystical illumination that I had ever had. It was in the form of warm, luminous thoughts that poured into my soul without any strenuous effort on my part. I was sitting in my room one late Autumnal evening in 1968,

---

[1] One of its most memorable lines is, *What is essential is invisible to the eye.*
[2] He had just founded the Friends of the Western Buddhist Order.

contemplating the various notes I had scribbled down about the opposing forces that brought about imbalance. *Who or what could bring about a healthy balance between them and have the ability to transcend them?* The answer came, in the form of another question, *Who or what archetypal figure contains both opposites within him or her - Reason and Imagination, Male and Female, Divine and Human? Of course, it has to be that mysterious figure which has accompanied me all my life, but of whom I had the only haziest of notions. Now it emerged into the full light of day, like a sun rising. It was the Being of Ultimate Love,* which is how I imagined Christ to be.

The next day I floated around in a state of exhilaration, wanting to tell the world of my discovery, but of course I realised no-one would understand, so I kept it to myself. I now experienced an extraordinary flowing together of different currents of thought and feeling, which I had been occupied with for years. *Yes, of course, not only is Christ the pivot or fulcrum of our soul, but He has to be the pivot in world history.* (At the bottom of the U shape I had described). *He appeared at a time when we had lost our connection with the Divine World. Only by uniting ourselves with this new cosmic power of love could we hope to re-ascend the path we had come down on, but now as free, creative spirits.* In a strange and unexpected way, these thoughts had the same limpid clarity as those experienced as a schoolboy on proving a theorem in geometry.

There was to be one more decisive encounter with another teacher in the staffroom, whose name I cannot now recall. He was even more taciturn than John who took me to the Buddhist talk. Most lunch breaks he would disappear off to the British Museum, where I learnt later he had been studying the ancient texts of the Cabbala.[1] One break however, I fell into conversation with him about an article we had both read in *The Observer,* and which I had cut out and put in a file. It was about psycho-analysis and behaviourism, - which we both regarded as one-sided forms of psychological understanding of the human being, - and the need for a more comprehensive picture. I was very excited about it because it confirmed my own, if less coherent thoughts about the matter. At the end of our conversation which was interrupted by the bell for the next class, he simply said, *You must read Owen Barfield.* I can't remember having another conversation with him for the rest of my time at the school.

Some weeks later, one Winter Saturday afternoon, I was browsing in Swiss Cottage Public Library. Suddenly a book leapt out at me. It was by Owen Barfield. That evening I devoured the book at one sitting. (I say 'devoured' because it was like appeasing a deep hunger). It was called, *Romanticism Comes of Age* and it was a collection of essays about the evolution of consciousness and the faculty of imagination as a way of knowledge. There was a lot I didn't understand – unfamiliar concepts about different kinds of souls and so on, but the overall effect it had on me was, *Yes, yes, that's exactly what I have been trying to articulate.* It was

---

[1] Jewish esoteric writings

a wonderful feeling of being inwardly confirmed. Someone else was thinking my thoughts, but taking them to a much profounder level. And here was my picture of evolution as a U shape, which I don't remember ever having seen before in any other writing. The work of poets like Shakespeare and Coleridge and Dante were explored as well as the philosophies of existentialism and linguistic analysis, but there was one thinker whom I had never heard of, who occupied a central place in the book. And this was someone called Rudolf Steiner. *Who was he? I must find out more about him.*

Some days later I saw a small notice in The *Observer* advertising a talk on psychology at Rudolf Steiner House. For some reason I did not take notice of the name of the speaker. All I was interested in was the fact that there was a meeting place named after Rudolf Steiner, so there must be a chance to learn something about him. Also the talk was on a subject I was interested in. A few weeks later I took the tube from Swiss Cottage to Baker Street which was just a few stops down the line, and walked back a few hundred yards to Park Road to where it was. I was intrigued by what seemed to me to be an expressionist façade of the building. With mounting spirits I went inside, only for them to be somewhat dampened by the gloomy interior. (Years later the interior design was made to be much more inviting). What had I come into? Was it some sort of spiritual sect? I looked around at the people there. They looked reassuringly normal enough. The talk was held in a small theatre. It turned out to be another of those 'peak experiences' for me. I could assent to everything that was said about the limited validity of both psychoanalysis and behaviourism and the need for a more comprehensive understanding of the human psyche. I don't remember now what was said in detail, - just an overpowering feeling of being yet again inwardly confirmed. The talk seemed to be very similar to the article I had read months previously in *The Observer* but took the argument further forwards. The speaker presented his case calmly and cogently but unlike many academic lectures I have attended, it wasn't read from a paper but spoken straight from the heart. At the end I was bursting with questions, but felt too nervous to raise them in an audience of about forty. It was announced that people were welcome to carry on the questions and discussion in a smaller room upstairs afterwards. Due to the shyness I suffered from at the time, I nearly went away, but I forced myself to go. I was immediately put at ease by the welcome given to me by the speaker. (I reflected afterwards how important these simple human acts are). He introduced himself. I said, *'Aren't you a writer?'* as the memory of his name began to surface to my consciousness. *'I write for The Observer'*. *'How extraordinary! I cut out an article of yours some time ago'*.

I don't recall the content of the discussion, apart from one of the questions that someone raised, which was whether Steiner's philosophy was compatible with Christianity. On hearing that it was, I remember feeling relieved. (Strangely enough, I didn't pick that up on reading Barfield's book, which on re-reading it, it is clearly evident). Talking to John Davy after the discussion, I learnt that he was now the Vice Principal of Emerson College, which was in Forest Row in Sussex. He explained that as well as having various training programmes in education and the arts, based on Anthroposophy, there was also a foundation year. *'Anthro-what?'* This was the first time I heard this strange unpronounceable word. He briefly explained what it meant. *Anthropos* - the human being. *Sophia* – wisdom. It could be rendered as *'An awareness of our humanity'*. He then went on to describe what happened on the Foundation Year – courses on the humanities, - literature, history, philosophy, religion, mathematics, the natural and social sciences, and the practice of various arts and crafts, as well as half a day working on the College biodynamic farm. *'What does 'biodynamic' mean?'* *'A form of organic agriculture initiated by Steiner'*. What had this man not concerned himself with? *'And do the students participate in all the courses?'* *'Yes. There is no specialisation in the Foundation Year'*. *'And are there exams'*, I asked nervously'. *'No'*, he laughed. *'Only in the training courses is there assessment, naturally'*. As he was speaking, my heart beat faster. It was as if a dam was slowly bursting. Here was a form of holistic education that I could only dream of, and inspired by a philosophy that I could feel confidence in. I just knew that I wanted to go there. It was arranged that I could look round the College and have an interview in June. I felt it was a long time to wait. (It was then February). But no matter. For the first time in years, Hope was returning. I was coming home.

A New Age dawning

I made friends with the man who had asked the question about Steiner and Christianity. Geoff was a tall, stooped figure, with a woolly beard and a large heart. His views on life were startlingly original and not always comprehensible to my rather limited Western intellect! He was deeply immersed in Sufism[1] when I met him. The only acquaintance with it that I had had up till then were the *Nasruddin* tales, which I used for English teaching purposes. Through him I learnt much more and found its teachings on awareness quite appealing. He invited me to take lodgings in his house in Kentish Town which he shared with his wife and three young children. I readily assented not only because of finding a kindred spirit but also the rent was much lower than I had been paying, thus enabling me to start saving up for the fees for Emerson College.

Now my social life radically began to change. A constant stream of all sorts of extraordinary characters would pass through his doors, with endless hospitality dispensed by his long-suffering wife. She was the archetypal Irish woman of peasant stock, who had a fierce common-sense which balanced out his rather wild and erratic behaviour. He was of Russian and Rumanian Jewish stock and could have stepped out of a Dostoyevsky novel. They couldn't have been more

---

[1] A mystical branch of Islam. A beautiful Sufi saying I came across later was, *The wound is the place where the light enters you.*

opposite. She was classic Taurean and he was Aquarian. (At the time I was learning all about astrology from my friend Robin). She had an immediate intuitive sense about people and situations, insights which took Geoff much longer to reach via a rather undisciplined 'mystical' route. In a sort of way, they reminded me of my Austrian friends, Mena and Hans with their opposite temperaments. (This is one of many recapitulated experiences I was beginning to become aware of, but on another level. I will try and say more about these in the last chapter).

Geoff earned his rather precarious living doing carpentry and building maintenance, and helping out his father in the art and antiques business. I think Maggie, his wife must have worried a lot about where the next pennies were coming from, but this didn't stop them both from being very generous with food and drink to anyone who dropped by. There were Sufis, Gurdieff followers and many young people who were at the end of their tether and who found solace in this unusual household. Life was never boring. I had never met such a colourful cast of characters before. Earnest and sometimes hilarious conversations would go on into the early hours of the morning. Geoff had a manic energy which bordered on what some people thought was mental abnormality. I didn't know what to think. But I did occasional experience him in states of hyper-awareness which could have mentally unbalanced him were it not for Maggie's ever-watchful and calming presence. Those times were not easy for his family. This could be reflected in the last lines of a poem written by his 10 year-old son, which I wrote down in my notebook of the time.

> *I wonder what every flower*
> *Does every day and every hour*
> *I wonder what made trees*
> *That everybody sees*
> *I wonder why men blunder*
> *I wonder*

In the same notebook, I also wrote down a poem that was given to me by an Irish poet called Madge who visited the house. It has such a rare beauty I will quote it here.

"The Horses" by Madge
> *Could I be sure*
> *They do not fling back their heads and laugh at me*
> *I would say to them*
> *Your Highnesses*
> *To the white horses*
> *Alas and I will never know*
> *To what strange field*
> *Their laughter ran*
> *If I'm above*
> *And they mount the air of 'Canabud'*
> *I will allow for each bird that shoots past my mouth*
> *Then come with me*
> *And away out of your mind*
> *To play with the white horses*
> *On the Banks of Thyme.*
> *They were young to die*

The horses in the sky
One had the world
Come up through His eye
And one drifted past like thistledown
They are beautiful
When they are in Rhyme
In Galway once
I met a man
He talked of horses
All the time

In the following months, Geoff and I would attend talks and discussion groups at Steiner House, and take out books about Anthroposophy from the library. The more I learnt about Steiner's astonishing insights, the more I became convinced this was 'the Gold' I had been seeking. Not only did I find an answer to my question in his book, *How to Know Higher Worlds* (although Christ is not directly mentioned there) *'Can there be a form of the Eightfold Path which can be related to Christianity?',* I also found confirmation of my other hunches, mainly in his book, *An Outline Of Esoteric Science-* that consciousness evolves, which can be depicted as a U shape; that there are two powers that create imbalance in our personal and social lives, and he names them as real beings, 'Lucifer' which literally means 'the light bearer', and 'Ahriman', the god of darkness, a name taken from the Zoroastrian religion. At Steiner House I was shown a picture of a large wooden sculpture that Steiner had carved at the end of his life, assisted by an English sculptress, Edith Maryon, It depicted these two beings held in check by a central figure called *The*

Representative of Man. At the top right of the sculpture was a strange small figure which he called the Spirit of Humour. I found that reassuring!

At the heart of history and within our own soul lies the reality of what he calls the 'Christ Impulse'. What particularly appealed to me was the fact his understanding went far beyond both the liberal and traditional notions of Christianity. It was both a cosmic and personal reality that one could also relate to other world religions. In extraordinary ways, which in these first few months I was just beginning to discover, he showed deep, mystical connections with the figures of Buddha and Krishna, and also with pagan wisdom. One of his first lecture cycles that he gave when he began to reveal Anthroposophy to the world was *The Bhagavad Gita and the Epistles of St. Paul.*

His books were not easy to read and there was much that I had no experience of, or had previously thought little about, such as reincarnation and karma, life between death and rebirth, and the existence of nine choirs of angels (although like a good Anglican, I heard the priest recite every Sunday as a boy,.. *And with the angels and archangels and all the company of heaven...* without thinking they were real or not!).

Although a lot of this was new to me, I was prepared to be open to its possible truth because so much else he said was an absolute confirmation of what I had discovered for myself. So it was not a matter of being converted to a new set of beliefs, but acquiring experiential knowledge. And what was not yet experienced could be regarded as thought experiments or hypotheses that could be tested in the laboratory of one's own heart and mind. And I suppose what was most remarkable of all, which up till then and also subsequently, I had not encountered, was the existence of a spiritual philosophy that could also be applied practically. But I am getting ahead of myself. It was really at Emerson College that I became aware of all this. But I did discover eurythmy at Steiner House. This was another exciting realisation of what I had been speculating about, - a dance to language. Eurythmy was an art of movement that Steiner initiated in 1912 and it purports to make speech and music visible. Through bodily gesture and movement one *sees* the words and music. Also, I was delighted to see a picture of the Second Goetheanum[1]– a huge sculptural edifice (one of the first large reinforced concrete buildings) that Steiner had designed to be the world centre of Anthroposophy. It was on top of a small hill in the village of Dornach, near Basle, sited against the backdrop of the Jura hills, whose forms matched its own. It reminded me of my favourite building, Le Corbusier's Chapel of Ronchamp.

It is difficult to convey the powerful emotions that I experienced coursing through my whole being at this time. As I have already said it was an overwhelming feeling of *coming home*; of recognising something you already knew. Writing this now, I am reminded of the last lines of *Little Gidding*, one of the *Four Quartets* by T.S Eliot, a favourite poem of mine at the time.

We shall not cease from exploration
And the end of all our exploring
Will be to arrive where we started
And know the place for the first time.

I also saw a picture of his first building, the 1st Goetheanum, made of wood, which was burnt down on New Year's Eve, 1922/3. This had been built by an international community of Anthroposophical artists, craftsmen and local builders during the 1st World War. It had a unique interior of painted ceilings, coloured windows and carved columns.

I tried to convey my discoveries to my two friends, Robin and John, but was met with raised eyebrows and glazed eyes, an experience I was often to have throughout my life whenever I tried to talk about them to various friends and family members. So one learned to moderate one's enthusiasm and keep a tactful silence.

During these last months in London, I got to know a woman who was introduced to me by my brother James. She was recovering from a long, unhappy love affair with a married priest, both of them dutifully upholding their Christian moral principles. She was now looking for a deeper spiritual understanding of herself and life generally, having rejected her formerly held notions of Christianity. This brought her to Emerson College a few years after I left. The artistic and educational insights of Anthroposophy she found quite inspiring (she had been a primary school teacher), but she now simply could not accept anything to do with Christianity. This subsequently led her to discover other Western and Eastern spiritual teachings which provided me with a challenge as to how I could relate them to my Anthroposophical perspective. From her I learnt that the Spirit is alive in many different guises. Eventually she became a Tai Chi teacher. She never found her life companion, but she managed to create for herself in London bonds of deep friendship with a wide variety of people, beautifully manifesting for me that love borne out of freedom, whose Spirit she could not acknowledge in its conventional name. I write about her here because of those qualities and also because she became one of the few close friends I have had throughout my life. She died some years ago.

In my impatience, June 24th, Midsummer's Day, the day I, (and Geoff) were due to visit Emerson College, seemed to approach very slowly. Around this time, a Greek student of mine offered to help me set up a language school in Athens. But I now knew what my next steps in life were to be, assuming the College would accept me and I could afford it.

John Davy had invited us both to stay with him on the 24th so we could experience Michael Hall, the local Steiner school's celebration of Midsummer, which was also St. John's Day. The next day we were to be shown round the College. The school was also in Forest Row, which was a large village not far from East Grinstead. The celebration started with Class 12 performing a play by Shakespeare (I can't remember which), followed by a chorus of other pupils singing something from Wagner's *Parsifal*, while processing to a large bonfire which they then lit with their flaming torches They hadn't done that sort of thing in my grammar school! Then as the fire got going, an imposing figure, whom I learnt later was the Principal of Emerson College, made an inspiring speech about likening the sparks that streamed heavenwards to our stale and uncreative thoughts that needed to be burnt away.

The next day we were shown around the College which was a few miles away at the other end of the village. It was the end of a long drive, - a large mansion surrounded by extensive grounds dotted with various wooden huts, and a large new building behind the main house. The whole site was a hive of activity – students painting, sculpting, making pots, doing eurythmy, reciting poetry, bookbinding, and engaging in activities I had not seen before - something called Bothmer gymnastics, a form of fluid physical movement, and projective geometry, which looked really beautiful. Here a lecture was being held, there a seminar. Behind the buildings were vegetable gardens, and further away a biodynamic arable and dairy farm, which provided the food for the College. There was a creative buzz in the air, the staff and students were friendly – I just knew I had to come there. I was interviewed by the Principal, Francis Edmunds, and it was agreed I could start in the autumn. I was granted a loan towards part of the fees. The rest I felt sure I could raise somehow. Geoff who came with me would have loved to have come as well but his family responsibilities had to take priority.

The next day back in London, my boss wanted to see me. My immediate thought was, *What have I done?* Nervously entering his office, I was greeted with a friendly smile and asked to be seated. *'The Deputy Head is retiring and I was wondering whether you would like to fill the vacancy'.* I was so taken back I was lost for words. Then I managed to say, *'Thank you for considering me but I was intending to come and see you this week to give in my notice.'* I explained why. It was certainly a positive note to go out on.

I was sorry to leave my students but it was a relief to emerge into the fresh air out of that somewhat claustrophobic school environment. There was one month before College started. I still needed more money for the course so I did something that normally I would never have entertained. I enrolled on a short course for selling encyclopaedias! The money was good as long as you managed to sell any. The product, beautifully designed, was aimed at children and was all about the human anatomy. The week's course consisted of learning a sales pitch by heart, from getting your foot in the door to persuading the hapless parent to buy the book. And you were taught various cues as to what to say when, and how to say it. It was naked manipulative behaviourism, the very thing I knew was wrong. But I swallowed my misgivings. *After all I was not asked to force someone to buy it. It was good value for money and it is finally the parent's decision.* But I didn't really convince myself. After our week's training, with a heavy heart I joined the bunch of other twenty somethings at Charing Cross tube station at nine o'clock on a Monday morning. Led by a young man not much older than us, we travelled to North London and were sent off to various areas clutching our precious product. We were to reassemble later that day after we had covered so many streets. It was a respectable middle-class neighbourhood, smug-looking 1930's houses with net curtains. My heart sank. *Knock firmly on the door or press the front door bell but not for too long, stand back a little and give a warm smile, not a smarmy grin or a nervous, uncertain look. When the house owner comes to the door, be polite and not pushy. While you are introducing yourself, take a glimpse into the hall and see if there are any signs of children. If there are, that's a good beginning.* Several times my offer was politely, or sometimes not so politely, declined. I was beginning to have a fellow-feeling for Jehovah Witnesses! Then at last, oh heaven! I was asked in and invited to sit down. I got halfway through my spiel and then dried up like an actor. The prospective buyer chuckled and said, '*You are new to this, aren't you?*' 'Yes', I said with great relief. '*Bad luck! I know what it's like. I was a salesman once.*

Good luck next time', and then he showed me the door. It was time to meet up with the other salesmen. None of us had 'made a killing'. *'Don't worry. It's always like that on the first day. You'll have better luck tomorrow, you'll see'* said our leader.

The next day we went to a different part of North London, in a similar sort of neighbourhood. Off we sallied forth like knights going into battle. This time after a few failures, I managed to step across the threshold. I remembered my script, when to pause and when to let them handle the precious product. *You mustn't let them hold on to it for long as it will disrupt your flow.* I got to the end and nearly, oh ever so nearly I got the victim, a woman, to sign, which would have meant her committing to a considerable amount of money. Then she hesitated and said she must consult her husband first. We were told if that happened, you would surely lose the prize. It was that last part of the sales pitch which I was particularly uncomfortable with. The whole thing was designed to lull the householder into a state where he or she could be easily persuaded to sign, which meant paying an instalment upfront. So I was relieved I hadn't made a sale! After some further rejections at the doorstep, I again was nearly successful, this time with a man, and reached the final stage. And then he said, *'I feel I am being pressurised to sign. I need more time to think about it'*. With great relief, I said, *'Do you know, I absolutely agree with you'*. We both went to the local pub and got thoroughly drunk. I composed myself as far as I could and staggered back to my fellow salesmen at the tube station. Everyone thought I had made a killing as I looked so happy. I sat next to the leader going back in the train and told him what happened. Strangely, instead of getting cross, he confessed to the same misgivings, but said he had to earn some money, having been out of work for some time. He found he had a talent for door-to-door selling and was eventually promoted to being a trainer.

Thus ended my glorious two-day career as a salesman. I can't remember exactly, but some financial arrangement was made with the College whereby I could pay off my fees in instalments.

The next few weeks before starting College was spent back at home with my mother. It was a chance to try and explain to her and my siblings where my life was leading me. Needless to say, there was no real understanding, but they noticed I looked much happier than before, so in that sense it must be a good move. It was different with my sister, Olga, who was training to be a health visitor. She showed great interest, and came to Emerson herself three years after I was there.

Emerson College Years (1969 to 1971)

The change in my life could not have been more dramatic. First of all, being in the country was like a great healing balm after living in a city for three years. Because the new student accommodation on campus hadn't been completed, I walked over the farmland from my lodgings in the village every morning and heard the larks singing, and looked up at the stars in the evening on my way home. It all brought back vivid memories of my childhood. I realised from adolescence onwards, how much more I had been enamoured of urban living than the rural environment I had been brought up in. On Wednesday afternoons, there were opportunities also to engage practically with Nature, helping out on the biodynamic farm or in the vegetable gardens.

My student accomodation

Secondly, now finding oneself a member of a thriving international community after all those bleak years since leaving university (apart from those moments I have described), was extraordinarily exhilarating. There were about eighty students on the Foundation Year, mainly from the Americas and Europe, and some from India and the Far East, with several from Britain, Australia and New Zealand. Most of them were in their twenties but there were quite a few who were much older. During the first week we all shared our stories of what brought us to the College. Reassuringly there were so many reasons why we were there, and also the fact we had come out of quite different cultural backgrounds. But all of us had recognised something in Steiner's work which put our life experiences into a deeper and broader perspective. At one end of the scale there was Jeff, a young twenty-one year-old American who had come out of the hippie scene. He dramatically and sometimes humorously, narrated to all of us his journey of spiritual awakening, from a very materialistic upbringing, to taking LSD, then becoming a Zen Buddhist disciple in New York, and after a spell in India, discovering Anthroposophy. In wonderful contrast to this story was Sandy's, a sober, middle-aged Scottish solicitor who had been impressed by his children's Steiner education and wanted to learn more about what lay behind it. It has to be said though, that there was a sizeable contingent of young, idealistic Americans that particular year, 1969, who were seeking new forms of community in which everyone should contribute their fair share. Some of them found it rather difficult however to carry out the various domestic tasks the students were expected to do, like washing up and serving meals. One social evening, a time when various forms of entertainment were organised by the students, a few of us put on a pseudo-circus sketch called *The Anthrobats* which gently satirised their idealism.

There were many who had come via an Eastern route, who wanted to reconnect with Western culture. Their particular challenge was to accept the central place accorded to Christ in Anthroposophy. And then there were others who called themselves Christians, who struggled with the idea of reincarnation and karma. There were also a few who remained generally sceptical throughout the year about Steiner's spiritual claims, but who nevertheless stayed the course like Steve, who was doing an MA on William Blake. And some had no particular spiritual or intellectual views but they were attracted by the general creative ambience, like John, an out-of-work opera singer who was visiting a friend and decided to stay. There were quite a number of artists and musicians who contributed to the general cultural life of the College. One such was a Scottish bagpipe player who wore a kilt – a delightful, eccentric fellow who loved to knit in lectures. He was a member of an obscure Celtic mystical sect whose name I cannot remember.

The third and most important reason why it was such a turnaround in my life was the fact that at last I was in an environment where all my spiritual and creative needs were being met, mediated not primarily through the study of books but through the enthusiasm of dedicated teachers who loved their work.

Looking back, they were a remarkable group of people whom Francis Edmunds gathered around him, some of them having been there since the founding of the College in 1962. All of them had such different personalities and temperaments and varied ways of working with Steiner's ideas. Francis Edmunds was an inspiring, fiery character – a typical choleric pioneer who led from the front. Of Armenian Jewish parentage, he had engaged in peace work with the Quakers, and then discovered Steiner education.

He was a short stocky man with a large, broad head and coal-black eyes which burned into your soul when you looked into them. He had a kind of coiled-up energy which radiated out through the whole way he spoke and  moved. After retiring at sixty-five from a lifetime of teaching, he intuited the need for centres of further education which addressed adults' spiritual and social needs. There were American funders who wanted him to start such a college in America, but for various reasons it was not possible and so it began in England, but keeping the original suggested name of the American thinker, Emerson. Ralph Waldo Emerson's philosophy of transcendentalism was seen as a 19th century precursor to Anthroposophy. Edmunds was good at lecturing whether it was on Anthroposophy as a whole or on specific subjects like education or science, but he was not so good in discussion groups or seminars. Again he was good at giving the overall inspiring motif of a play he was directing (usually it was a Shakespeare) but not so much with offering individual suggestions to his actors.

His lectures on Shakespeare were particularly enlightening. He regarded all the plays as a whole, - a progressive revelation of Shakespeare's consciousness - an approach which I had not come across before. One of the varied courses he gave which stays with me was one about teaching physics to young people. He said in Steiner schools, physics begins with the study of acoustics. And you don't start with talking about wavelengths, which is a theoretical construct, but with *an experience* of sound. And then with a flourish, he threw back the top of the grand piano and asked us to gather round with our heads almost inside the piano, to listen to the sounds that were created by holding down the notes of an octave, a fifth, a third and others, without playing them. This meant those notes without the damper on them could be free to vibrate when the first note in the series was played with a quick, short touch and the loud pedal down. Then we were asked what other sounds we could hear. It was like a bit of magic, - the harmony of the spheres. He explained it was the overtone series that we heard which every note contains. This series actually contains all the notes of a scale but spread out over many octaves. Normally one can only hear the octave above the note played, and the fifth above that. He then explained that later in subsequent lessons he would teach the children the science of it all, e.g. about the ratio of the length of the string to the sound that was produced. Science in

Steiner schools would always start with the children observing the phenomena first before going into the theory. This meant they would be fully engaged with their senses before purely exercising their intellect. This has the effect of arousing the pupil's interest in what can be for many of them rather remote and abstract subject matter. In Anthroposophical terms he said it was bringing the warm enthusiasm of Lucifer to the cool logic of Ahriman. I could have done with that in my science lessons at school which were deadly boring and tedious! The way art is introduced in Steiner schools the opposite happens. There are a lot of disciplined colour exercises in the primary school years before individual originality is encouraged. This leads some visitors to Steiner Schools to remark that many pupils' paintings look the same. The same people though would not complain of music students all having to play the same scales to achieve musical competence, yet that is what colour practitioners need to do – practice their 'scales' to achieve greater colour sensitivity.

John Davy, the Deputy Principal, with his modest demeanour and calm, clear thinking was a good balance to Edmund's more rhetorical and imaginative flourishes. (Yet another example of the Dionysian/Apollonian polarity).

In contrast to him, he was a

John Davy

Emerson

tallish, lean figure with a small, narrow head, not unlike Ralph Waldo Emerson's, whose portrait hung up on the college staircase. John was particularly good in group work with his capacity to listen to a wide variety of views

146

that was a hallmark of the student community, and then relate them to a bigger picture. Having worked on *The Observer*, he was in touch with English intellectual and cultural life and was very keen on bringing in other people to the College to give talks or run seminars,- whose ideas were arrived at independently from Steiner's. Such a person was Ernst Schumacher who made a great impression on me with his practical proposals for an Intermediate Technology and also a Buddhist form of economics.

There is one 'imagination' that John gave which I shall always remember. He painted a picture of a new kind of 'Fall' in our age, - a fall of human knowledge. The human being is understood as an animal, the animal as a plant, - (a bio-chemical entity without an inner life of feelings and treated or rather maltreated as such in factory farming where it is not allowed to express its essential nature of being able to move); the plant as a complex set of chemicals to which other chemicals are applied, such as artificial fertilisers, herbicides and insecticides; and even the solid world of the mineral has been reduced to a lower level in atomic fission, with a highly toxic outcome. I would add now to what Davy said, - that in fact you could say that 'poison' or sickness has been created at the other levels as well. If humans are treated like creatures of instinct, or 'a head on legs', whose behaviour is to be manipulated and measured by reaching targets and outcomes, then it is no wonder they fall ill; if animals and plants are exploited as food-producing machines, it is not surprising diseases occur.

Our present-day sciences have reduced reality to a purely physical dimension and you could say, even further to a set of mathematical equations. There is nothing left but a phantom. It is like giving accurate measurements of a number of footprints without realising they were produced by living beings with feelings, and a sense of purpose. This reductionist, analytical form of knowledge is of course perfectly valid when it is applied to the physical, mineral world, like building bridges or performing surgery, but becomes inadequate in relation to the living world, let alone to sentient forms of life.

The social sciences are reduced to biology, which is reduced to biochemistry, which is reduced to physics, which is reduced to mathematics.

John Davy argued we need to reverse this 'Fall' by developing higher forms of knowledge and understanding appropriate to the nature of the phenomena that is being studied. And here he introduced us to the scientific work of Goethe, the German poet and naturalist, whose qualitative approach to natural phenomena, (a 'delicate empiricism' as he called it) was the foundation of Steiner's spiritual researches. Through what he calls 'exact sensorial imagination' that is, through careful and systematic observation of the phenomenon, e.g. the continually changing forms the plant manifests in its life cycle, he was able to build up within his mind a series of successive images of it, unfolding *in time.* The matching of this dynamic mode of thinking and perception to the living nature of the phenomenon it was being applied to, enabled him to 'see' the 'invisible essence' of the plant, which he called 'the archetypal plant' *('ur-pflanze')*, shaping its forms into visibility. Goethe claims that this is a direct perception, not a thought-out idea. It is interesting to note that when the word 'idea' was originally coined by Plato, it meant in Greek, *'to be perceived'*. (Something that was not pointed out on my philosophy course). Only in the last few centuries, has it, and the word 'concept', become to mean a purely mental construct. So again, but now consciously, it is possible to experience thinking as an organ of *perception*. Through what Steiner calls the faculty of Imagination ('image' or 'time' thinking), we can begin to see the creative forces working into the realm of space out of the world of time. Just as it would be absurd to look for the cause of the magnetic needle moving, in the needle itself, because it lies in the magnetic nature of the earth as a whole, so is it equally absurd to look for the causes of the seed sprouting or the embryo taking shape within the physical phenomena themselves. They have to be sought elsewhere beyond the physical world. We learnt in the introductory talks at the College on how biodynamic agriculture works, for example when seeds are planted, the position of the moon and the planets are taken into account, - something that the old peasant farmers knew intuitively. This was a good example of how a concept or hypothesis taken from Anthroposophy, or Spiritual Science as sometimes Steiner called his work, could be tested *physically*. Seeds planted when the moon is waxing have been shown repeatedly to grow more vigorously than when the moon is waning. Knowledge arises only when there is a union of concept and percept, of thinking *and* perceiving. Concepts only, produce speculative philosophy; percepts only, – the amassing of data without an organising theory, - lead merely to unrelated bits of information, the curse of our times. I will mention later the seminar work we did on Steiner's book, *The Philosophy of Freedom.*

Through various other courses based on Goethe's approach at the College, I began to see that practising this kind of 'perceptual' thinking has important consequences for our social life. We are less likely to unfairly pass judgement on others if we imagine them in a *process of becoming,* - that is, they have had a past, which we may not know about, and they also have a future, that is, a potential which we can't see at the present moment. Judging them at a particular cross-section in time is like saying the plant *is* the seed or *is* the leaf.

One of these courses in what could be called 'Goethean phenomenology' was John Wilkes' class, where he got us to model the gradually changing segments of a cow's backbone in clay. In doing this several times one became aware of what happens in the gaps, between each shape. It was as if the invisible was becoming visible. (John, a professional sculptor, through observation of how water naturally flows, was later to develop forms cast in concrete, which allows the water flowing into it, to move in lemniscatory loops (figures of eight). This has the effect of not only oxygenating the water but enhancing its 'life-forces'. It is being used successfully in reed bed sewage treatment. This is a good example of art fructifying science).

I enjoyed all the courses that were on offer, doing things I had never done before. Pottery with Ann Druitt began with the students digging up their own clay. I made a book in Lionel Elin's class, which I have only now decades later, filled with poems I have written over the years! I experienced more of eurythmy with Elisabeth Edmonds, wife of Francis, a highly sensitive artistic soul, and practised the forming of speech with a rather intense, melancholic young man, Graham Ricketts. This was developed by Steiner and his wife, Marie Steiner towards the end of his life, at the request of actors and speakers of epic and lyrical poetry who were seeking for an enlivening of their art. It aims to find a balance between the Apollonian form found in the articulation of consonants, and the Dionysian nature of the vowels which express feelings. The secret lies in the right flow of breath and a heightened imagination of the gestures that the sounds of language make in the air, - shapes that eurythmy makes visible through movement in space.

For the first time ever I managed to paint something which I didn't want to throw away in disgust. In Ann Stockton's classes we used the wet-on-wet method where water-colour paint is applied to paper that is soaked in water. With careful brush strokes, the colours almost form by themselves into shapes you choose. They can be abstract or semi-abstract expressions of feelings, or more representational shapes. All this is gradually led up to by first becoming attentive to the 'inner gesture' of single colours, e.g. red tends to approach you, blue recedes, etc. Through concentrated practice, we learned the 'language' of colour. In my case the end result was not necessarily 'art' but the process of doing it, I found quite therapeutic. A polar opposite to this sensory experience was Olive Whicher's projective geometry classes. Here one experienced the pure discipline of creating all sorts of shapes out of points, lines and planes without using any measurement. One learnt to think imaginatively, in turns of polar opposites, which at the same time was subject to a beautiful form of logic. For example, a line can be thought of being created by the intersection of two planes as well as something that is formed by joining up two points; or a point can be thought of as the intersection of three planes instead of being created by the crossing of two lines; or a circle formed by tangents coming in from different directions from the cosmic periphery, as well as a form made by radii coming out from a common centre. Dizzying notions of going through infinity and coming out the other side were demonstrated with great elegance and clarity. Steiner had suggested that this form of non-Euclidean geometry could be applied to understanding the changing dynamic forms of growing organisms where the cosmic peripheral forces of levity operated as opposed to the earthly forces of gravity. This was something Olive Whicher was developing but it was too advanced for us Foundation students. Olive also taught us what is called Bothmer gymnastics because it was developed by Count Bothmer along the ideas of Steiner as a suitable form of physical movement for children. It involves flowing, rhythmical movements arising out of an imagined world of levitational forces peripheral to the physical world where gravity operates, not unlike the ideas behind projective geometry. It was a joy to behold our beloved teacher demonstrating these various movement exercises with youthful enthusiasm. A short, compact lady in her fifties, she looked as if she herself was formed out of all those peripheral planes coming out of infinity!

Another course I enjoyed which had to be held when it was dark, was stargazing with John Meeks. We learnt to identify the constellations and the legends that lay behind them.

I have not yet mentioned the morning lecture courses and the seminars that followed them. Many of the young Americans didn't like the lecture format, but I couldn't have enough of it, because many of the talks confirmed what I had conceived in only the barest outline, that is, the evolution of consciousness, but now immeasurably deepened. The ones that particularly stayed with me all these years later were 'the magical mystery tours' as we students called them - a pictorial voyage through the millennia looking at the art and architecture of Ancient Egypt up until the present day, as expressions of spiritual evolutionary processes.[1] This was led by William Mann, a retired teacher at Michael Hall. An even more extraordinary story of the human being evolving from a purely spiritual state to the physical being we are today, was given in John Davy's lectures. It gave credence to the old myths and legends of our origins but now in an evolutionary perspective. It was just a matter of reading in the right way their symbolic meanings. Steiner had once remarked that Anthroposophical research findings would not have been possible without Darwin's evolutionary hypothesis, even though he

---

[1] See **Endnote 2**

derived different conclusions from them than Darwin did.

Another course I hugely enjoyed was given on the history of English literature by Cecil Harwood. He was one of the original 'Inklings', the literary and philosophical group around C.S. Lewis in Oxford in the twenties. It included Tolkien, the poet Charles Williams and Owen Barfield. Harwood went on to found the first Steiner school in this country, which began in London and then moved down to Forest Row. Now retired, he brought a delightful flavour of the old days of Oxbridge academia with him, including the tobacco smoke that curled upwards from his ever-present pipe! I relished his profound knowledge of literature delivered in such a genial and objective way. My hero, Owen Barfield also came to lecture but it was a disappointing experience. He seemed to lack the knack of public speaking. I managed to take the opportunity of thanking him for the decisive effect his book had on my life.

There was one visiting lecturer, Adam Bittleston, whose singular appearance and manner of speaking, made a great impression on us students. He was a very tall, stooped figure in his fifties, with long uncoordinated arms and legs, youthful, rosy red cheeks and owlish spectacles, and an extraordinary, long drawn-out manner of speaking, which held one spellbound. He had a captivating impish, almost Sufi-like sense of humour which sparkled through his rather diffident manner. His main themes were Christianity, and how one could understand what 'The Word' could possibly mean, as expressed by St John; the spiritual significance of Shakespeare, counselling and Celtic spirituality, which influenced the nature of the prayers that he wrote for personal use. He was the Principal of the Seminary of the Christian Community Church in Forest Row, which gave the foundation of a priests' training before they continued it in Stuttgart.

The Christian Community was founded in 1922 in Germany by a group of mainly ex-Lutheran priests, theologians and students, who were looking for a renewal of Christianity appropriate to this age, having been inspired by Anthroposophical Christology. They asked Steiner for advice as to what form a new way of worship and priesthood could take. To their surprise, Steiner suggested a renewal of the seven sacraments. It was to be a church with a strongly contemplative element, free of formal dogma and centred on the sacramental life. Its priests would be both male and female. Steiner was emphatic that it was not primarily meant to be a church for Anthroposophists, but for anyone who was seeking for religious renewal in their own lives and in the life of society. Steiner's own particular task in life was the foundation of a *science* of the spirit, not establishing a new religion. It was another *application* of Anthroposophical insights, in this case to the religious life, just as there are to other spheres like education and agriculture. My impression was when I attended a communion service, was that it seemed to be a kind of combination of Quaker and Catholic spirituality, - Quaker in that it involved *a silent contemplation* of the ritual that was being enacted by the priest and the servers, but without the personal bearing of witness; and Catholic in that the priest wore vestments and conducted the four stages of the mass, and giving an address, but without pronouncing any dogmas to adhere to. And there was incense too! I found the words quite beautiful and profound, and spoken with reverence and artistic sensibility. The celebrant spoke with quiet conviction and the various ritual movements he made were performed as if he knew why he was doing them. Sometimes, I experienced in Anglican services that the priest either said, sung and made gestures that looked as if they were done automatically and without inwardly feeling the meaning of them, or at the other extreme, the emphasis was on preaching, either emotionally or intellectually, and the service lacked any aesthetic coherence. This Catholic/Protestant tension is of course at the heart of Anglicanism and occasionally, I have witnessed it being resolved and lifted to a higher level. Then I wished (this was mainly in my adolescence) that there could be a church with that kind of balance (not the middle-of-the road between 'high' and 'low' church kind of dull blandness), but a dynamic blending of beauty, meaning and significance, in a church which is not beholden to the State, as the Anglican one is in this country.

Here again I experienced another 'miracle' of confirmation of feelings and half-formed thoughts that I had had earlier on in my life, in this case concerning religious practice.

I discovered later that Adam Bittleston became a good friend of William Golding when they were students at Oxford, and their friendship lasted all their life. Golding did not become an Anthroposophist but some of the ideas did percolate through his novels.[1] It is said his friend formed the basis of the character of Nathaniel in his novel *Pincher Martin*, - a portrait of a man *who is simply good, eccentric, physically uncoordinated and utterly trusting.*

Another memorable visiting lecturer was Alex Podolinsky, a biodynamic farmer from Australia, a tall, lanky, forceful character who claimed he could *hear* the sun rise – in an A major chord. It was a matter of debate for us students as to whether he was imagining it or that he really was clairaudient. After all it was known to the Ancients that such a possibility existed of being able to hear the *Music of the Spheres*. Perhaps it was not just a fanciful metaphor after all but a genuine perceptible reality.

There were many other courses but I have restricted myself to relating those that still linger in the memory after over forty years.

The day was so structured that lectures were held first thing in the morning when you were supposed to be fresh and alert (I don't think that applied to all the students!), to be followed after a morning break of coffee and all sorts of herb teas which were quite novel at that time, and seminars and study groups on some of Steiner's basic texts. After lunch it was a good time to be active in other ways, when the processes of digestion make us less mentally alert, so accordingly that was the time for courses in the arts and crafts.

---

[1] A modern novelist who openly did declare his debt to Anthroposophy was Saul Bellow, featuring it in his novel, *Humboldt's Gift*.

One of the texts we studied was *The Philosophy of Freedom*, an early work of Steiner's, which was a theory of knowledge and a foundation of ethics. Surprisingly, I did not find it easy, probably because it seemed to be very much like the philosophy I had left behind at University. It has taken me some time over the years to really *experience* the validity of what he was presenting in a purely philosophical form, which he said became the basis of his later spiritual researches. He argued that you have to become aware of the role thinking plays in our acquiring knowledge of the world, as I mentioned earlier. The active influence of this hidden element in our soul life is now much more recognised in the current field of consciousness studies. The section on ethics was immediately more comprehensible. An act can only be truly called moral if it issues out of freedom and love, thus disputing straightaway Kant's dictum that morality must be based on duty. (Steiner had studied Kant as an adolescent and knew from experience that he was mistaken, particularly in regard to Kant's argument that there are human limits to knowledge. Kant makes a distinction between the world of phenomena that is accessible to our senses and intellect, and the world of what he calls *noumena*-'things-in-themselves', - which is not accessible to our mind and senses. This is the realm of religious *faith,* which we cannot have *knowledge* of. This dualistic picture of the world goes way back to the Middle Ages, and is still around today as an unconscious assumption we carry around with us. Steiner already knew from his visionary capacities of perception as a young person that there is ultimately only *one* world, - the non-physical or supersensory element, the 'frozen tip' of which, is the material world. *At our present stage of consciousness* it remains inaccessible to our normal faculties of perception. If we develop higher organs of perception, traditionally called the 'chakras' or 'lotus flowers' in Eastern esoteric wisdom, then it becomes able to be experienced. In his book *Theosophy* he gives the example of a blind man trying to understand the seeing man's experience of red. The redness of an object is in the same space that the blind man is in. It is not in a separate world. It only appears to be so because the blind man has not the requisite organ of perception to behold it. So likewise we are in the same position as the blind man when a seer such as Steiner describes spiritual phenomena to us. In our case though, we do have the means to acquire new faculties of vision if we follow a particular meditative path.

But that is half the story. An appropriate form of thinking needs to be developed too, as I have already described earlier in relation to Goethe, which relates these spiritual 'percepts' into a greater organism of knowledge.

To come back to the subject of ethics, we are only truly moral, Steiner argues, when we act out of a free intuition and a love for the action itself. We have to *want* to do the action out of an intuitive understanding of what is necessary in that particular situation, not an abstract reasoning of what can be realised universally as being the foundation of ethics, - the so-called 'universability' principle of Kant. He, Kant, argues that to perform a moral deed, you have to act so that the basis of your action may be valid for everyone.

In Steiner's understanding, the less constrained we are by our natural instincts *and* also by the demands of duty in so far as we follow them out of unthinking social convention, the freer and therefore the more moral we can become. It is not a matter of whether the will is free or not, which has occupied thinkers down the ages, but crucially whether the will can *become* free. (It is interesting that a neuroscientist has said recently that it looks as if science has once and for all proved that we do not have free will, but if we examine our actual experience in overcoming a bad habit through acquiring *knowledge* of the consequences of persisting in following such a habit, e.g, smoking, we can modify or even change our habits completely. We have exercised our free will in spite of what the theory may say.)

Here is a quote from *The Philosophy of Freedom.*

'When Kant says of duty; *"Duty! Thou exalted and mighty name, thou that dost comprise nothing lovable, nothing ingratiating, but demandest submission,... thou that settest up a law... before which all inclinations are silent, even though they secretly work against it,"* [1] then out of the consciousness of the free spirit, the human being replies: *"Freedom! Thou kindly and human name, thou that dost comprise all that is morally most lovable, all that my humanity most prizes, and that makes me the servant of nobody, thou that settest up no mere law, but awaitest what my moral love itself will recognize as law because in the face of every merely imposed law it feels itself unfree"* This is the contrast between a morality based on mere law and one based on inner freedom.'

---

[1] Critique of Practical Reason

Most of us are still *evolving* to be free spirits, so social standards of morality still have some justification. Only we cannot acknowledge them as the absolute standpoint in morality. To quote, *Nature makes of us merely natural beings; society makes of us law-abiding beings; only we ourselves can make us free beings. At a particular stage of our development nature releases us from her fetters; society carries us a stage further; the final touches we must apply ourselves.*

Finally, I would like to quote a sentence from the Preface which really describes the touchstone by which all forms of knowledge, spiritual and practical, need to be measured by. *Knowledge has value only in so far as it contributes to the all-round development of the whole nature of the human being.*

Another text we studied was *Theosophy* which I have already mentioned. (It is a term which simply means *Divine Wisdom*, - a name that was used in earlier times such as in St. Paul's Epistles or in Jacob Boehme's writings). Here Steiner reinstates the notion of the Trinitarian[1] nature of the human being, - that we are a unity of body, soul and spirit. In ancient cultures and in early Christianity, this was known about. The body was the perishable part; the spirit was the part of you which neither died nor was born – your immortal essence; and the soul mediated between the two. It could either go the way of the physical body or be raised to the level of the spirit. Gradually from the 9th century onwards this understanding got lost and dualism took its place. The

---

[1] He also reaffirms in other books the ancient insight that this human trinity is a reflection of the Divine Trinity. See Appendices **3** for a poem I wrote about the soul and **4** for one about the Holy Spirit.

realm of the spirit became external to us, mediated by a priesthood and only to be believed in, not known. We now just have an outer 'objective' part, - the body, - which science investigates, and an inner subjective part, - the soul. Ethical, religious and aesthetic values and beliefs are purely personal, - a matter of opinion. And just at the time when a further reduction was taking place, at the beginning of the 20th century – to being just material bodies, the rest being an illusion, - Steiner claimed, out of a direct perception, and not out of philosophical speculation, that we do indeed exist in 'three dimensions' which form a unity when we are alive, but separate out when we die. The physical body disintegrates, the soul and spirit continue to exist in their own worlds and follow laws of development which he describes in detail. I shall only describe here what sense it meant to me then. If there is life after death, and of course there's no way of scientifically proving it, then his descriptions seemed to make better sense than the rather vague speculations of liberal and progressive Christians, or the literal interpretations of hell, purgatory and heaven found in traditional doctrine.

Put simply and briefly, he said that in order to progress morally and spiritually, we need to experience how we affected others while on earth *as if we were them.* This experience of becoming aware of the consequences of what we say, think and do, makes our 'higher self', our spirit, resolve to meet up with them again in a subsequent life on earth, where we have another chance to make amends and move forward. It is a form of judgement, but it is not by a fearful father figure of a god, but by the Divine within us. (Of course most of us in this present stage of human evolution are blissfully unaware that we have this task to do. However, unconsciously our destiny brings us together with the people we are connected with from past lives. It is up to us what we make of what we are given).

Also in this 'Soul World', called *Purgatory* in the Christian tradition and *Kamaloka* in the Hindu one, we need to be gradually weaned off our various earthly attachments, whether physical, psychological and even religious (in so far as it was determined by our cultural inheritance), before we are ready to pass on to the world of the Spirit, which in Christian terminology is called *'Heaven'* and in Hinduism, *Devachan*. In this blissfully creative realm, helped by higher beings of an angelic nature, and ultimately by Christ, we prepare for our next life on earth.

It all made sense to me, but at that age I wasn't too preoccupied with such matters! Some thirty years later I wrote a song to be sung at my mother's funeral, accompanied by my nephew, Nicholas, on his guitar. It includes a few descriptions that I have left off in my narrative above, namely that for the three days after death, our 'body' of life forces gradually leaves the physical body.[1] This releases all the memories of what

---

[1] Another picture that Steiner gives of the human being is a fourfold one. We live in four 'dimensions' of being: a physical, spatial one which we share with the mineral world. This is the only one that can be perceived by our physical senses; an 'etheric' one of growth processes in time, which we share with the plant world; an 'astral' one of instincts and basic soul processes which we share with the animal world; and our 'I', our uniquely human identity, out of which unfolds our Spirit.

happened to us on earth, - spread out like a tableau. People who nearly die say they have seen their whole life flash before their eyes. Also in the soul world we go backwards through our life experiencing what we have done to others, until the moment we were born. And then we enter the spirit world. This gives another interpretation of what Christ says, *'Except you become as little children, you shall not enter the Kingdom of Heaven.'*

.

Imagine – a song

Imagine a world where no thing is
Imagine a space that's inside out
And a stream that flows backwards

For the first few days you see your life
Spread out like a tableau before you
And now your great soul journey begins
From the moment of death to your birth

But here you're on the receiving end
Of all that you've said and done
This makes you resolve to meet once again
All those with whom you're connected
In future times to make amends

And in this purifying fire
You let go of earthly attachments
Made ready to pass to higher spheres
Of blissful activity

And all the while you're with people you love
Those souls that have gone on before you
Guided and helped by angelic choirs
And enfolded by the Being of Love

The other text we studied was *How to Know Higher Worlds*. This is a manual of self-development which includes not only the Eightfold Path, but many other kinds of concentration and meditation exercises. The ones that particularly appealed to me then and still do, were those which involved heightening of our senses, such as looking and listening to natural phenomena[1]. Stilling the chatter of our own minds we allow the various sense impressions, of colour, sound, shape etc to impress themselves into our souls, and then allow the feelings arising from this, to resound on within us. This has the effect of temporarily re-uniting us with Nature, overcoming that gap between us and the world, which I had been feeling so acutely in my twenties. Reality is not 'out there' as present-day knowledge would have us believe, and the inner world is 'maya' – illusion; neither is it the other way round, as some Eastern mystics say, - that the external world is 'maya'. What *becomes real* is our conscious participation in all the processes of life, and that requires heightened attentiveness and the employment of our capacities for imagination. As I have said earlier, we need our imagination to fill in the gaps between what we can observe with our senses, e.g. the growth of a plant. Steiner gives the name of 'Imagination' to the first stage of a higher form of perception and

---

[1] I wrote a verse about this recently. See **Appendices 5.**

knowledge. *How to Know Higher Worlds* shows one how to develop it. I have to say it has taken me decades to even take the first steps!

In the evenings there were rehearsals for plays and concerts, social events, special talks and presentations. I took up flute playing again and sang in the college choir. It was led by a great enthusiast, Brien Masters, who was the music teacher at Michael Hall. The main piece we worked on and performed at Easter was Bach's *St. Matthew's Passion,* which was an extraordinarily dramatic and moving experience. For four years since leaving university I hadn't had the opportunity to act. Now it was possible again. The first production I was in, was an English mediaeval mystery play followed by *The Tempest*, both produced by Francis Edmunds. Here I played *Stephano*, the drunkard. Of course I wanted to play Prospero but I was no match for John, the opera singer, who had a magnificent voice and a build to match. We had a wonderful costume designer, Roswitha Spence, who had been a professional before she came to work for the College. She had evolved a way of design through a 'Goethean' approach to colour, shape and texture. Through making phenomenological studies of the characters and the scenes they were in, we expressed their 'soul moods' as she called them, in colour, form, and texture, using pigments, materials and clay. Out of all those playful exercises, designs emerged that were sensory expressions of soul realities. For example my character demanded rough-textured material and muddy brown colours, whereas Prospero's character was expressed in long-flowing, finely-textured robes, coloured purple and gold. She also worked with ways of emphasizing the various parts of a costume, e.g. a low waistline, or a high neck collar, to indicate traits of character. I used these techniques in my productions later at the Merlin Theatre and found them to be very fruitful as starting-points for design.

The first term seemed to stretch into infinity. Everything was so new and exciting. In the next term one began to cast one's thoughts forwards to the future. *What should I be doing next?* The passing of time began to be a reality! And the third term shot by. We were asked to undertake a project of our own choosing. I researched into the origins of music, which entailed consulting ancient manuscripts in the British Museum.

Various people came to visit me during my first year at Emerson, including Robin who remained sceptical of it all. Despite the esoteric nature of Anthroposophy, he simply couldn't accept its Christian aspect. He left the Language Tuition Centre a year later, fell in love with a Danish woman and moved to Denmark. I was not to see him again. Marie came in the spring and loved what she saw. She decided to come as a student two years later. My sister, Olga who was a nurse and health visitor, also decided to come as a student after visiting me. She attended three years later. My Mother also paid me a visit, accompanied by Otto and Eileen, his wife. The only comment I remember my Mother making about the visit was the ghastly taste of the dandelion coffee that she drank!

Students were now deciding whether to leave or enter a training in Steiner education or one of the arts. I think about a quarter decided to stay on.

I was in a dilemma as to what to do next. Subaramu, a mature Indian student whom I had become friends with, invited me to his Gandhian teacher training college in Bangalore. He was the Principal and he thought I could be of some assistance. It was very tempting but I thought I needed to prepare myself further in what I was gradually becoming aware of what it was I wanted to do. And that was in the field of adult education connected with the arts, particularly drama. It would be a cultural centre offering similar life-affirming experiences that I had been privileged to have while at Emerson, but now made more accessible and affordable in an urban setting, where I knew from experience there was a desperate need.

Now the time came to say our fond farewells. For many, like me, it had been the best time in their lives. Never had I been in a situation before where all my philosophical, spiritual, and artistic passions flowed into one, as well as my love for making things in the craft sessions – something I hadn't done since my childhood.

Most of them dispersed to other sides of the world and I would never see them again, but there was one with whom I had made good friends, and have kept up contact until the present day. And that was Mike Preston, who was seven years my junior. On discovering Anthroposophy when he was twenty one in his home country of New Zealand, he immediately decided to come to Emerson. He had an exuberant energy and generosity of spirit that I put down to his pioneering ancestry, alongside a fine-tuned sense of the absurd, which I found quite appealing. Over the years, our intermittent contacts gave rise to one of the few deep and lasting friendships that I was blessed to have, - the kind of relationship in which one could share the more intimate aspects of one's inner life as well as converse on all manners of subjects, particularly philosophy, the arts and religion, and at the same time try and keep a humorous perspective on it all. Mike decided to go into teaching, and trained as a Steiner teacher as well as a State teacher. After some years teaching in both kinds of schools, he obtained a Masters in education and philosophy, and then later a PhD in the phenomenology of perception with Merleau-Ponty and Wittgenstein as teachers and inspirers. For the last twenty seven years he has been teaching in Steiner schools in the States.

What was to be my next step? How would I realise my dream of being involved in an urban cultural centre, or help create one, as I didn't know of one such existing in Britain? I felt I needed a training in Anthroposophically-oriented drama skills which I could use in such work. The problem was, - no such training as yet existed in Britain, (unlike those in eurythmy and the visual arts). However there were several students like me, as well as a few professional actors in the local neighbourhood who felt the same need. We got together and asked Francis Edmunds if we could pioneer such a course ourselves, bringing in various teachers to help us. This request touched a nerve in him. It had been always one of his ambitions to have such a training course at Emerson, so we were in luck! He asked us to come up with a curriculum, which he would advise on too. Our foundation would be the Speech and Drama Course which Steiner gave to a group of actors in the last year of his life.[1]

We managed to secure the help of Graham Ricketts who could further our vocal skills; Elizabeth Edmunds to give us eurythmy as a meditative movement path; Ursula Koepf for Greek Gymnastics which Steiner said was good for developing inner mobility of voice and gesture. All these teachers were on our doorstep. We also acquired the overall theatre skills of Peter Bridgmont, a professional actor and director living in London, who was developing some of the practical suggestions in the Speech and Drama course. These various classes formed the basis of our training, to which we added our own studies and work on various theatre texts. Looking back on it now, it seems astonishing the College managed to find the resources to fund such an enterprise, because I don't think the fees we had to pay could have covered it all. I worked in the holidays teaching English as a foreign language to pay for part of it. The rest I was allowed to pay off in the ensuing years.

The new academic year started well enough. There were ten of us with an equal number of males to females of varying backgrounds of theatre experience. We all felt privileged to be the pioneers of such a course in Britain. By the second term however, cracks began to appear in our very different approaches to theatre, basically

---

[1] It seemed extraordinary that at a time when he was beginning to be seriously ill, that he should have found the energy to do this, alongside lecture courses to doctors and theologians, sculpting his figure of Christ, further work on meditation and karma studies and much else besides, including countless private meetings with individuals who had come to him for spiritual help.

splitting along the archetypal lines of what could be called the Apollonian approach, which emphasizes the virtue of the discipline of objective form, manifesting particularly in the art of speech, and the more anarchic, Dionysian element in the art of gesture. Marie Steiner, the actress wife of Steiner, had developed the former since her husband's death in 1925, and trainings arose out of her work, but very little had developed in the latter sphere. (However there was someone whose approach became prominent decades later, and this was the work of Michael Chekhov[1], Anton Chekhov's nephew. He had been a famous actor in the Moscow Arts Theatre who had trained with Stanivslasky in the twenties. He broke away from him by developing his own methods influenced by Anthroposophy which he had begun to work out of, years later. If we had worked with his approach, it could have provided the necessary balance between our one-sided leanings towards the one bias or the other. (I leant more to the Dionysian). As it was, the gap between us became more unbridgeable and the course faded out in the last term, much to everyone's disappointment, not least Edmunds'. However I think we learned a lot about ourselves and the inherent difficulties of being the founders and at the same time the students of an artistic training together. Some of us went on into professional acting, others took up teaching. Peter Bridgmont proceeded to do the full speech training which had just been established in London, after which he founded his own drama school

---

[1] Chehkov eventually settled in America and taught many Hollywood actors like Yul Brynner and Marilyn Munroe. Through their connection she began to take an interest in Anthroposophy.

in Balham. I was determined to carry on training where I could. I made the acquaintance of Ann, a German 1st year student who told me about her experiences of attending an Anthroposophical drama therapy school in Stuttgart run by a Frau Schneider. She, to all accounts was a remarkable woman who had evolved her own methods of correcting the various bodily and psychological imbalances of ex-drug addicts and others, through movement, song and speech. This sounded like a possible next step.

While pursuing my drama studies in 70-71, I also had time to take part in college productions, including *Thor with Angels,* a powerful poetic drama of the Fifties by Christopher Fry, whose work had fallen out of fashion since Osborne and Pinter began to dominate the English stage. I also continued doing pottery, playing music and pursued my own private studies.

One was of Steiner's early life[1]. I found it somehow reassuring that he had fully entered into the spirit of the age, particularly while he was in his twenties in Vienna, studying natural science at the Technical University and afterwards, meeting all sorts of people, avant-garde artists, poets and thinkers, often in the thriving coffee bar milieu of the time; and in Berlin some years later, directing plays, and lecturing at a working man's institute.

---

[1] Apart from Steiner's own autobiography, I read later Emil Bock's lively account of his early years in his *Life and Times of Rudolf Steiner, Vol 1.* There is also a fascinating first-hand impression of him in his Viennese years given by the Austrian novelist, Stefan Zweig in his book *The World of Yesterday.*

While fully engaging with very different and often opposing world views,[1] he was gradually forging his own and at the same time quietly developing his inner meditative life. It was near the turn of the century that he felt ready to make public the results of his spiritual researches, including the truths of Christianity, which up till then had been closed to him.

At the same time I made a study of Steiner's social and political ideas expressed in his book, *The Threefold Social Order.* He argued that the cultural, political and economic spheres of society need to each become autonomous and self-regulating. Theocracy, state socialism and conventional shareholder capitalism, blur the natural boundaries between them and tend to result in tyranny, inequality and unfairness. Harmful influences would include, e.g., corporate pressure on governments, state attempts to interfere with science, education, and religion, or religious influences on organs of government. He restored the French revolutionary ideals but differentiated them. The cultural realm (science, art, religion, education, and the press) requires and fosters freedom; the political (and legal) realm, equality; and the economic realm, uncoerced cooperation and solidarity.

This attempt to reconcile the competing claims of individual cultural freedom with social and economic justice, mediated by a new democratic political life of rights, became a mass movement which emerged in

---

[1] One that he had a lot of sympathy for, was the work of Franz Brentano, whose lectures on philosophy and psychology he attended at Vienna University. Brentano's ideas could be said to be the direct ancestor of phenomenology and existentialism.

Germany after the First World War. If it had found political expression, which it very nearly did in Southern Germany, it could have prevented the rise of Hitler. However the fierce opposition from both Left and Right stopped that happening. Steiner's life was threatened by Nazi thugs after an address he made in 1922 to thousands of car workers in Munich. The 1923 Beer Hall Putsch in Munich led Steiner to give up his residence in Berlin, saying that if those responsible for the attempted coup [Hitler and others] came to power in Germany, it would no longer be possible for him to enter the country. In 1919, an industrialist called Emil Molt asked Steiner for advice for setting up an educational programme for the workers in his cigarette factory in Stuttgart. By the workers' request these educational methods were then applied to their children. Thus the Steiner School movement was born. It became very popular and other parents not employed by the factory, and also in other German towns, asked for such schools to be established. In 1933 when the Nazis came to power, they were closed down, but by that time they had spread to other countries.

Various people visited me in my second year, including Catherine Sare, as she was then, a friend of my sister's, who had just finished a degree in landscape architecture. She was looking for a new spiritual orientation in her life, and her visit led to her enrolling the following year. She became a good friend and we have remained in touch until today. After a year at Emerson, she trained in Vienna to be a eurythmist, and finally ended up becoming a eurythmy therapist working in an Anthroposophical medical centre allied to a NHS trust in Maidstone, called the Blackthorn Trust. Steiner had suggested various speech sounds in relation to various ailments which the patient could practice in eurythmy, which under the direction of a qualified doctor and in combination with other artistic therapies, would have a healing effect. David McGavin, a medical doctor who also had trained in Anthroposophical medicine[1], founded the clinic, gathering around him a group of therapists working in colour, music and eurythmy. Together they have achieved success in treating a whole host of ailments, particularly in the fields of chronic illness and latterly, pain control. It has won a number of awards for integrative medicine in the community and Dr.McGavin became NHS Doctor of the Year in 1993 for his work in mental health.

Another visit I had towards the end of the year was from my eldest brother David/Father Bernard, who had just been expelled from South Africa after encouraging too much contact between the white and coloured students at Stellenbosch University where he had been woring for two years. One day he had been listening to a Prime Ministerial speech in parliament when suddenly he heard his and a fellow monk's name mentioned as being unwelcome guests in the country. He could well have said *'these meddlesome priests'* as Henry the Second was supposed to have said about Thomas a Beckett! In the next few days they had to pack their bags and depart. There was no possibility of legal reprieve.

After my first year at Emerson, I had sent him a tape which tried to convey my joyful discovery of

---

[1] See **Endnote 3.**

Anthroposophy, and the experiences I had there. I found I couldn't express it all in writing, so I thought it would give a more direct picture if I spoke it all out aloud. Unfortunately the tape machine didn't work properly so he only got a rather mangled account. So when he got back to England he must have wanted to check it all out, to see if it was not some strange cult. He asked if he could borrow a few books from the College library. He chose Steiner's lecture course on *St. Mark's Gospel* and *Theosophy* which he had for a few weeks. He didn't say much about them when he returned them, but it felt as if he had been reassured that it was not unchristian! In the following years however we were to have some animated discussions about the nature of Christianity.

It was near the end of term. A small group of us who were interested in contemporary classical music and where it was going, went to London to hear Stockhausen talk about his music. The lecture hall was overflowing so we had to see him on a video screen in another room. The lecture was technically very demanding and I understood very little. Afterwards we managed to fight our way through the crowd of adoring acolytes and ask him about his more meditative compositions. *Ah*, and his eyes lit up, *I was acting the German professor tonight! You would like to hear more about that side of my work?* And then he proceeded to talk about his studies of esoteric Christianity. His whole manner and appearance was a wonderful emblematic expression of his split musical personality. He was immaculately dressed in a dark suit with a tie but with a hippyish ponytail. In the academic musical world he was fêted for his intellectually complex atonal compositions but they were completely perplexed by his 'New Age' spiritual music. It was a fascinating glimpse into the cultural revolution that was happening in the beginning of the Seventies, a kind of cosmic battle for the soul of the artist. We left with the question, *Is there another dimension beyond these two kinds of music which the composer (and the listener) can draw on?* I was becoming more convinced that the future of all the arts, not only music, will demand a conscious inner change of how we perceive things, - see, hear etc. Perhaps it will take a few centuries before all the old forms fade away and a new Renaissance occurs.

During the whole of my second year I went out with a fellow student, Vivien, who had been brought up in Chile, of English parentage. She seemed to have adopted the sunny nature of her Latin American compatriots. She had an enthusiasm and zest for life which I found quite captivating. She was in her second year at Emerson, on the Steiner education course. Unfortunately our lives had to take different directions after college. She had an offer of work in the Mexican City Steiner School, and I felt I had to continue preparing for my hoped-for future, although I have to say I was tempted to go with her to Mexico! (Thirty or so years later, I met her in England, now married with two grown-up children, and it was not long after that I attended her funeral. She had died of cancer.)

Finally I had decided I would study at the Schneider Schule, although I didn't relish the thought of staying in Germany again. I would need to do some English language teaching throughout the summer to earn some money. A week before the end of term, Edmunds offered me a free ticket which someone had donated, to the week-long summer festival of all four Mystery Plays by Steiner at the Goetheanum in Switzerland, which I couldn't refuse. I was interested to see them, as well as his building and sculpture.

Soon after leaving Emerson I made my way to Dornach, a large village not far from Basle. The Goetheanum could easily be seen on top of the hill overlooking the village. The pictures I had seen of it, did nothing to prepare me for the experience of the sheer scale of its sculptural masses. Apparently it influenced Corbusier in his later work, and also Kenji Imai, the Master of modern Japanese architecture.

The performances were a unique theatrical experience, the likes of which I had never had before! The stage was huge, the lighting and live sound effects were stunning, and the speech choruses of spiritual beings were 'out of this world'! Unfortunately however, my German wasn't up to fully understanding the more intimate (but long!) dialogues of the human characters. By reading summaries of the plot in English and attending the accompanying English lectures about the plays, I managed to get some idea of what was going on! It is basically about a group of characters who suffer various ordeals and setbacks in their search for self-knowledge. You see them in the 20th century first, then some of them with changed gender, in their previous lives in the Middle Ages, in the early Christian centuries and in Ancient Egypt. Their thoughts and actions in earlier lives are seen to be influences on their behaviour in later ones. I was to see them performed again years later in English, and then they naturally made more sense. They don't display the dramatic skills of a Shakespeare, as I'm sure Steiner would have been the first to admit. They are the first attempts in world literature to depict such realities and I can imagine centuries later there will appear other dramatists who will be more advanced in their artistry, just as Shakespeare was, compared with the Mediaeval Mystery plays. The scenes which I find most dramatically worked through, are those in *The Ordeal of the Soul* which depict the conflicts between the Catholics and the Knights Templar in the Middle Ages. They appear together again in their present life, but now on a shared quest.

While I was there, I got talking to a young man with a Yorkshire accent, who was cleaning the main steps of the Goetheanum. He pointed out to me a group of people in the distance who had come from Sheffield, and said they ran an interesting theatre. I was so set on my next steps, which was to study in Germany, that I didn't approach them and introduce myself. It turned out that they were the people I would be working with the following year. Obviously I wasn't meant to meet them then.

* * * * * * *

Now began my drama course just outside Stuttgart. It was late September and cold winds blew straight off the Russian Steppes, as I walked to the school across the fields from the tram stop. Being more used to the milder English autumn, I hadn't brought adequate clothing. I was kindly lent a thick overcoat by Frau Schneider. There were three of us from Emerson, - John, the opera singer; Miriam, an American Jewish flautist, and myself.

The rest of the class, about seven of them, were young Germans, whom I gradually discovered, had come there to find a psychic balance in their lives. Frau Schneider was a middle-aged lady with a shock of silver hair and a very bright and clear, if not sharp, way of speaking, which I was told was typical of Berliners. She had undoubtedly developed remarkable powers of observation and was able to suggest various exercises we could do to re-adjust any physical and psychological imbalances that were revealed in the way we moved and used our voices. It was not easy for the three of us who were struggling with the German. Also we didn't feel the same need as the other students felt for personal therapy. John left at half term and Miriam and I struggled on till Easter.

It gradually became clear to me that in some strange way, I had to go through another German ordeal although it was very different from my first one seven years earlier, and I was also in a different place in my life. I say 'ordeal' because the whole experience was (still!) a challenge to my English soul which I felt unable again to completely surmount. The first was the difficulty of mastering the language; the second, their directness of manner which I still found difficult to get used to. (My failing, not theirs). More specifically, in relation to the course, I realised I would need another year at least to become teacher/therapist using these methods myself. I saw they worked but I didn't see myself in the future as a specialist. I still had the idea of becoming an adult educator using drama as a medium of expression.

There were compensations to my stay in Germany. One was getting to know my landlady, from whom I rented a very small room. She was an elderly Italian Anthroposophist who taught the piano in a most imaginative way. I was allowed to watch one of her lessons. Before the pupil was permitted to touch the piano, he learnt how to throw a ball to his teacher with ease and grace. Believe it or not, it is not as easy as it sounds. Then with piano lid closed, he was taught how to lower his spread-out hands as if ready to play. Then when he finally did press down the actual keys, after so much inner preparation, the experience was that much fuller and richer. She couldn't have been more opposite to Frau Schneider. Both of whom were highly developed artistically and spiritually. The latter was of large and ample stature and her speech was very formed and seemed radiated with white light, while the former was frail and diminutive, and her German was spoken with a soft, musical lilt and filled with colour. Being around her you felt bathed in her exquisite sensibility. Ugliness in any shape or form, - moral or aesthetic – was naturally repelled by her presence. I could imagine a Michelangelo carving a marble figure of Frau Schneider, but *she* would need to be *painted* by a Raphael!

Another highlight of my stay was teaching English to a group of adolescents in the original Steiner School in Stuttgart, which I did for a few hours each week to earn some money. This was my first experience of being in such a school, and the contrast could not have been greater than those I'd had, of being first a pupil and then a teacher back in England. First of all, the building itself seemed friendly, with flowing colour on the walls; no noisy, long and featureless corridors; no smell of stale milk (!), and like Emerson, there was a positive buzz of creative energy around the place. The students I taught were eager to learn and had a natural sense of easy self-confidence, which I had so painfully lacked at that age.

Miriam and I left the school at the end of the second term. We decided before we went our separate ways back home, - she to America and me to England, we would spend a couple of weeks together travelling around Italy. First we were in the Italian Lakes where we stayed with an Italian family. I was so taken with their custom of playing the lyre to their children before they went to sleep, and waking them up with recorders, I vowed that if ever I had children, I would do the same! Accordingly when the time came, eight years later when Judith, my wife, became pregnant, I asked an instrument-maker friend of mine to make a lyre for me. Unfortunately the opposite happened with our daughter, Hannah. When I played it, she became more lively and awake!

We spent a glorious week in Florence over Easter, which is celebrated in a unique way. A huge, decorated wagon is dragged through Florence by white oxen until it reaches *Basilica di Santa Maria del Fiore* in Florence's historic centre. Following mass, the Archbishop releases a dove-shaped firework propelled along a wire which sets off the planned firework display on the cart, followed by a parade in medieval costumes. This exotic experience, together with feasting on the art in the Uffizi gallery, and visiting a variety of beautiful churches, was a welcome relief to the rather ascetic and sparse existence we led in Germany.

* * * * * * *

I came back to London to an uncertain future but determined still to find the work I was looking for, but not knowing where to look. Geoff and Maggie Orson were kind enough to put me up again while I sorted myself out. I immediately found work as an EFL teacher, this time in a smaller school in West Hampstead. There I had two curious experiences. One was of the principal, whose whole manner, particularly his intense dark eyes, reminded me so strongly of the principal of my last language school and like him, tried to persuade me to stay on when I decided to leave. The other strange incident was talking to two other teachers at the school, who revealed they knew quite well three people from my nearest and not-so-nearest past. One was good friends with an old schoolmate of mine, Vince Guy, who studied PPE with him at Pembroke College, Oxford. He also knew John, the opera singer who went to Emerson. And when I asked his friend who had lived in Chile, whether he knew a girl called Vivien Osborne, not of course expecting an affirmative answer, he said he was best friends with her brother. Was this an example of happenstance, synchronicity or karma? I have no idea, but it did feel as if each one of us is at the centre of a web of hidden connections and for me this experience somehow betokened a gathering up of old karma, and a promise of new beginnings. (Seven years later, I had a similar sort of experience. Within the course of one month, I came into contact purely 'by chance' three old friends whom I hadn't seen since university days, - June, whose name I saw in *Resurgence* magazine; John Nettles, who was acting in a play at the Crucible,

Sheffield's professional theatre; and Jeremy Hooker, whom I learnt was an English lecturer at Aberystwyth University. This led for a time to a renewing of friendship, which was not sustained in the long run. What the significance of such experiences is, I have no idea, unless they are merely 'time echoes' or biographical 'after images'. Do others have them?)

Round about this time, I began to be aware of strange parallels of what immediately preceded and followed my time at Emerson College and my recent time in Germany and what immediately followed it, with my previous time seven years earlier immediately preceding and following my time at University, and then in Germany and Austria, and what happened shortly after. But now it was on another level, - what could be said to be on 'a higher octave'. I shall attempt to describe this and other patterns and rhythms I have become aware of in my life, in the last chapter.

Being in London again and teaching, was like going backwards in my life. It was beginning to feel claustrophobic. Then I heard, - I can't remember from whom,- that there was a job going in the Anthroposophic Press in Spring Valley, New York State. It was a secretarial post with opportunities to be involved in theatre work in the evenings and weekends. It was a community of various enterprises all inspired out of Anthroposophy, - a press, a biodynamic farm, a school and artistic and educational courses for the general public. It wasn't exactly what I was looking for. I was really wanting to be in the middle of a town or city, but as I was so desperate not to carry on where I was, I decided to apply, convincing myself that this could well be the nearest I could get to realising my ambition. I received a favourable reply from Gilbert Church, the managing director. I would need to learn how to type, which I started to do. Then a whole series of strange 'mishaps' or 'accidents' occurred which seemed to conspire against me from taking on the job. In a letter Gilbert Church sent to me weeks later, seven reasons were listed as to why things went wrong, including letters not being replied to in time because he was away on holiday and a date on a letter was misread by him; a letter of his not reaching the post-office; and a misunderstanding about my being expected to apply for a permanent visa. Then we talked on the telephone to try and resolve matters. But it still wasn't clear. However I thought I would go anyway and see if things could be sorted out! So I booked a flight to Kennedy Airport, New York and told him when I would arrive. A week before my flight, I went home to see my Mother, and started preparing for the trip. Then two days before leaving, I went down with a serious bout of 'flu. I was ill in bed for a week. The flight was not insured and I had no more money to buy another ticket. It felt like *Someone* was trying to tell me something!

Now what should I do? While at Emerson, I had done voluntary work for two weeks at Botton Village, a Camphill Community for adults with special needs. I was impressed by its general ethos. The villagers as they were called, were treated with dignity and respect, and they contributed to the economic and cultural life of the community by producing craft objects such as dolls, pottery, and wooden toys that could be sold to major retailers. Some of them also worked on the farm. There was a rich cultural life which all members of the community participated in.

The Camphill Movement was founded by Dr. Karl Koenig and other Jewish Anthroposophical doctors who fled to England from Austria just before the War. While interred on the Isle of Man, they came up with the idea of initiating a different way of educating what were called in those days, handicapped children and adults. It would be the complete opposite to what many people felt about handicapped people. The extreme form was taken by the Nazis in their homeland where they were beginning to be exterminated as useless and inferior members of society.[1] So it was an extraordinarily radical proposal, quite against the prevailing spirit of the times, that Koenig and others, implemented after the War. The first community and school for children with special needs was established in Camphill, near Aberdeen. The founders were inspired by the educational, medical and social insights of Steiner as well as those of Robert Owen, a 19th century social reformer.

I thought I should look into the Camphill training programme in Aberdeen to see if that could be a possible next step for me, as the American option seemed to have closed down. A friend was about to visit a friend of hers in Sheffield. I asked if she could give me a lift. There I thought I could see what was going on at the Merlin Theatre, about which I had the haziest of notions, before

---

[1] In a way it could be argued that they were putting into practice what so-called enlightened spirits in the West had already advocated in theory, decades earlier. We conveniently forget that Social Darwinists like H.G.Wells, G.B.Shaw and Dalton in this country, also thought they should be eliminated, through sterilisation and a eugenics programme of selective breeding.

making my way further up North to Aberdeen. It turned out that the friend lived a road away from the theatre. It was a leafy inner suburb two miles from the City Centre, quite unlike what I had experienced when I had visited my brother in Sheffield in the fifties. I walked down the drive to a large Victorian house set in beautiful grounds and saw to my right a most unexpected sight – a many-sided building made of light limestone blocks, with a multi-faceted roof. It reminded me of something. Yes, of course, the Goetheanum in Switzerland! I suppose I had been imagining a small, plain brick-built edifice in an industrial environment!

I knocked on the large wooden door of the house and was greeted by another unusual sight – of a small, frail-looking, youngish-looking man with a lop-sided posture and one lame arm. His eyes twinkled merrily through his large spectacles, with a thick mane of black hair flopping over his face. He introduced himself as Christopher

Boulton, and led me at a slow pace into the large kitchen to meet May, his wife. She looked ten or so years older than him, a silver-haired woman in her fifties, who must have been something of a beauty in her twenties. Their warm, friendly manner immediately put me at ease. For the next few hours, joined by May's brother, Norman and his wife, Janet, we talked non-stop, sharing our respective stories. It turned out to be the most unusual 'job interview' I had ever had! I explained what I was looking for, and they gave me a history of their initiative – how they began the work of Tintagel House and later the Merlin Theatre, and explained the symbolic and mythic significance of these names.[1]

Because so little is known about the origin of their work in Sheffield, I shall give here a detailed resumé of what they said in my own words, with some details that I learnt subsequently. The four of them were the founder members of the initiative, with others coming to work with them for shorter and longer times, plus numerous volunteers. Their tasks and responsibilities were various. Christopher devised the cultural programme of educational and artistic events, gave lectures and directed plays with the Merlin Players, a community drama group attached to the theatre. May was the 'mother' of the house, offering a warm welcome to anyone who dropped in, freely dispensing physical and spiritual nourishment. Many a young person in particular was helped to find his or her feet with her words of wisdom. Norman, a surveyor by profession, was responsible for maintenance, stage lighting and set

---

[1] See **Endnote 4**

construction. Janet helped out with administration. In a way, you could say they all made up one person, because they all had various forms of physical 'handicap'. Chris's was the most severe, having been struck with polio as a child; May and Norman both suffered from serious bouts of asthma, having been brought up in a working class area of Sheffield which was severely polluted. In addition May had TB in her twenties which weakened her constitution. And Janet had scoliosis. Before founding Tintagel, they were involved in the work of the Sheffield Educational Settlement, out of which their present work grew. This had been a unique and continuing experiment in adult education and community theatre founded by Arnold Freeman in 1918 in a poor area of the City. He had come from a wealthy family, and after Oxford University, wanted to devote his life to the education of deprived people, fired by the social ideals of Fabian Socialism. He came to Sheffield and began his work funded by his own resources. Growing dissatisfied with the limited outlook of his political ideals, he soon came across the work of Rudolf Steiner[1] whom he met before the latter died in 1925. This more comprehensive picture of the world he brought more and more into the lectures he gave on politics, economics, history and literature (he was a polymath!) and his audience were mostly those who had left school at fourteen and who wanted to improve themselves. Many of them found themselves drawn into plays that he directed in the tiny theatre which was part of the Settlement. It was really two back-to-back houses

---

[1] See page 206

joined together. He made no concessions there – only the classics! He was one of the first to put on Ancient Greek tragedies in Gilbert Murray's translation. Another essential ingredient of the work was the vibrant social life, which led to life-long friendships. When Freeman retired in 1954, a small group of Anthroposophists were determined to carry on the work. However they felt they did not have the unique gifts that Freeman had, nor the necessary financial resources. It looked as if the whole enterprise would come to an end. However a young man providentially appeared on the scene – who with his considerable artistic and spiritual talents, as well as his financial means, enabled it to continue. Christopher's background could not have been more different from May and Norman's, whose father was a steelworker. Because of his delicate physical health, he was tutored privately in Switzerland and the South of France. His father was an actor turned diplomat, and his mother was a well-born lady of means. From an early interest in Theosophy, he then discovered the work of Rudolf Steiner whose work addressed the questions that Theosophy didn't. Through a circuitous route, he was led to Sheffield and made an immediate connection with the group there, and there and then decided to commit his life and financial resources to their work. It was left to May to educate him in the ways of the Northern working-class world, particularly in the realm of money!

Seven years later, the area designated with demolition, so they moved to where they were now. The social and educational work continued but there was no theatre, which they knew from experience was a wonderful way for people to express their creative gifts and develop new ones, as well as giving the opportunity to forge friendships. Another seven years passed before their dream of having a theatre became realised. An American great aunt of Chris's, died childless and her legacy came to him as the sole remaining heir. It all sounded like a fairy story! The money came through in instalments, which enabled the small building team over two years, with Norman as clerk-of-works, to erect a 200-seater theatre at the bottom of their garden. Architectural plans had already been drawn up by an architect friend of Chris's - Kenneth Bayes, who was inspired by Steiner's design principles, - just in case they should ever have the funds to build it.

The theatre opened on April 23rd, St George's Day and Shakespeare's birth and death day, with a production of Shakespeare's *Henry the Fifth* by the newly-formed Merlin Players. For the next three years, Chris was engaged in a punishing schedule of productions, aided by a young couple, who designed and made the costumes and scenery. A few months before my visit, they had left to work in New Zealand and Chris and the others were looking for someone else to help them in their work. Could I be that person? At the moment, they had no spare room but in January, 1973, four months from then, the room would become vacant. *Would I consider coming to work part time then, until either side felt it could be made into a permanent post?* It felt like a kind of engagement proposal! They couldn't pay much. They operated on the Camphill model of living from a common pool of money, each receiving what he or she needs out of the common consciousness of what was possible. It didn't seem to me to be too different from

Marx's dictum, *From each according to his abilities, to each according to his needs.* Food and rent were provided, as well as the use of the Charity's car. I felt alright about this form of remuneration. I was always uncomfortable with being paid wages. During the end of my time working in London, I had the crazy idea of holding my hat out to the students and asking them to pay what they felt I needed to live. Needless to say, I didn't have the courage to carry that idea out! I was heartened to find my intuitions confirmed in Steiner's social and economic philosophy, in the sense that he said that in the future there would be a very different attitude to remuneration for one's labour. Now the whole system of wages is the last remnant of slavery. Instead of buying the whole person, one is still buying or selling one's labour. In various Anthroposophical institutions, including Camphill and this one, attempts have been made to find a different way. All have in common the arrangement that you get paid *before* you work, to *enable* you to do the work, not be rewarded *after* you have done the work. This attitude engenders trust and gives dignity to the worker. Apart from the money invested in the work by Chris, they earned their keep by renting out rooms to tenants and hiring out facilities to other cultural and educational groups, including now other local amateur opera and theatre groups.

I didn't have to make up my mind there and then. If the Camphill idea and any attempt to revive the American possibilities didn't work out, I would be welcome to contact them again and take it from there. I liked their free and generous spirit, and their attitude that Anthroposophy is there to serve the needs of others, and not something to be possessed for oneself.

I left with much to think about. Was this to be my life work, - a vocation, - as I couldn't regard it as an ordinary job? I would have to wait till January. It was now early September. What could I do until then, if other options didn't work out? (May told me much later that I looked as if I was in a kind of dream when I was with them that morning. A matter of walking unconsciously into my destiny?!)

I caught a coach to Aberdeen and had an interview. I was shown around the school and it soon became clear to me that this was not the work I wanted to do. Apart from more studies, I didn't really relish the idea of living and working in a community away from the city, despite the admirable nature of their work. That evening I celebrated my 29th birthday in an Aberdeen pub, feeling somewhat sorry for myself. I knew from my studies of the seven- year phases of life that 28/29 was the time that you finally feel the need to get stuck into something after the literal or metaphorical wanderings of the twenties. And that certainly applied to me... but whither?

As I was so far up North, I thought I would take the opportunity of visiting Iona. I had heard much about this sacred isle, from where Celtic Christianity spread into England and the rest of Europe. I was lucky to find simple accommodation in the famous Mrs Black's farmhouse on the island. Many a young pilgrim was put up by her. I was not to be disappointed by the magical atmosphere everyone said it had. There was something quite special about the quality of light after the rather glowering dark mountains of its larger, neighbouring island of Mull, which you had to cross in order to get there. Iona was like a glittering jewel with its white sands and beautiful green pebbles. I was moved by the simple, sturdy abbey and the remains of earlier settlements and the thought of St Columba and his twelve monks engaged in their dedicated work of prayer and the illumination of scriptures. The extraordinary Book of Kells was begun there. The next morning I got up before sunrise to walk up the small hill of *Dun I*, which I was told was sacred to the Druids. In the growing light I had the most powerful experience of thoughts pouring into me unbidden, - about the quality of light and the nature of the changing shadows, as the Sun rose above the horizon. I had never before, or since felt thoughts as living powers that seemed to grow within me like a plant unfolding in the light. Some years later I came to repeat the experience, but it was not to be. It was like a kind of Grace which had to be sufficient for one lifetime. I later discovered that Steiner had said out of his clairvoyant investigations into ancient history, that the Greeks experienced thoughts rising in their consciousness with the rising of the Sun in the sky. Now we experience thoughts isolated in our head. Then we participated with our thoughts in the processes of Nature. They were embedded in the cosmos. Well, perhaps I slipped back for a moment into my Greek incarnation! Whatever it was, I departed a few days later buoyed up by the experience, but still in a state of unknowing about my future. I learnt later that my brother David received his divine calling to be a monk while at a retreat in Iona. Nothing like that happened to me, nor did I expect it would. However what I experienced on *Dun I* was a most precious gift of the Spirit of Iona that lingers in my memory right until now.

I arrived back at Geoff and Maggie's in London with two letters waiting for me. One was from Gilbert Church, (which I have kept till now) profusely apologising for the mess-up of the arrangements we had tried to make, saying he doesn't customarily operate like that. This was the letter of the Seven Reasons which I have already mentioned. He ended his letter by saying I was still welcome to come and we could see if something could be worked out. The other one was from Chris and May saying that the tenant had left and there was now a room for me if I wanted to come up and join them in their work. Like waiting for a bus that never seems to come, suddenly two turn up. That seems to be a strange law that operates that when you have really wanted something for a long time, - two choices suddenly appear out of nowhere and you have to opt for one. Well, I knew which bus I wanted to take! I had never before tried so hard to convince myself of a particular course of action, namely going to America to work, but in the back of my mind really knowing I didn't want to do it. It seems you have to make as much effort as you can to achieve a goal, which somehow has the psychic or spiritual effect of clearing a blockage in your life path, but the outcome is quite different from what you expect in your conscious mind. Or to put it another way, the angels help whoever helps themselves. Or to put it in yet another way, your feet, rather than your conscious mind, lead you to your destiny.

A week later I moved up to Sheffield and immediately became involved with the planning of the Michaelmas festival which is on September 29th. There were about fifteen in the Anthroposophical group and a programme of poems, stories and music was prepared – all on the theme of the Archangel Michael (pronounced in three syllables, like Raphael). Michael is a being who is particularly connected with the Anthroposophical stream of spirituality. Since 1879, he has become the Guiding Spirit of the Age. The other six archangels each in turn lead humanity into a different kind of consciousness for roughly of a period of over 300 years.[1] Michael does not lead, but lets us free to respond to the call of the Spirit. Only then does he accompany us on our journey of initiative, enlightening and encouraging us. The Michael Age is marked by the development of 'heart' thinking and courage in our actions. Unlike the traditional images of him *slaying* the dragon, his task is to help us *tame* the negative forces inside and outside us, get to know them thoroughly and begin to *transform* them into a higher good. His festival falls in the autumn when our inner nature needs strengthening just at the time when all around us, outer nature is dying. Steiner describes it as a *potential* resurrection of the *human soul before* death in contrast to the Easter Festival at the opposite time of the year in springtime, when we celebrate the resurrection of the *body of a Divine-Human after* death. For me it was a beautiful polarity within the rhythms of Spirit and Nature. These two festivals remind us of the ancient doctrine of *divinisation* held by Paul

---

[1] See **Endnote 5**

and the early Church Fathers such as Augustine, Clement and Athanasius. The Divine becomes human so that the human can become divine. The Michael Festival celebrates our spiritual *potential* in preparation for the Birth of the Spirit within us at the Winter Christmas Festival. There's another polarity at the Solstices. Three days after the Summer Solstice on June 24th, when the *physical* sun is beginning to wane, the Festival of John the Baptist is celebrated (now mostly in Scandinavia). John, the last of the pre-Christian initiates, used physical means to awaken his disciples, that is, through complete immersion. In those days some people's souls had a looser connection with their bodies, so through a sudden shock, like immersion in cold water, they entered temporarily into a body-free consciousness. This enabled them to have a whole survey of their life in front of them. This is a kind of judgement leading to a state of *metanoia,* a change of heart and mind, which is the true meaning of the word *repent.* (As I have said earlier, people who nearly die drowning or falling from a great height often report that the whole of their life flashes in front of them). John points to a One greater than him who is to come after him and who will be the new spiritual Initiator of mankind. His Festival is celebrated at the opposite time of the year, three days after the Winter Solstice, when the light of the physical Sun is beginning to increase.

These festivals provide creative opportunities to re-unite Nature, Art and Religion, and also the participants, at a higher level of being.

* * * * * * *

To begin with, as agreed, I worked part-time for the Centre, augmenting my income with giving English lessons to a Japanese professor of politics I was introduced to. I helped out with various practical tasks, working front of house in the theatre or in the coffee bar, cleaning etc. My main involvement was in the current production of Macbeth that Chris was directing, - taking on a small part, coaching people in their speeches and helping out backstage during the performance. It turned out to be one of Chris' least harmonious productions. The part of Macbeth was taken by someone who insisted his partner play Lady Macbeth. Because he was the only one who could play that role, Chris had to give in to his 'blackmail'. She couldn't remember her lines and had to have two prompters either side of the stage. The couple who made the costumes did a bad job and delivered them late. I witnessed for the first time Chris' outbursts of anger which in a way were quite justified. The play certainly lived up to its unlucky reputation!

Despite this rather harrowing first ordeal of my new life, I decided I would like to work there fulltime, which they readily agreed to. This was now mid-November. The play came off better than expected, greatly helped by the visual impact of its design. Chris then asked me to direct the *Oberufer Shepherd's Play* (translated into English) for the Christmas Festival. This was one of a cycle of German Mediaeval Mystery Plays, discovered and revived by Professor Schroer, Steiner's teacher at Vienna University. Because of their refreshingly direct simplicity, Steiner recommended them to be performed to children. I gathered a cast together, mainly fellow Anthroposophists, including a few who had acted in

Freeman's day. This was my first production so I naturally felt a little nervous about whether I could make a good job of it. I was quickly put at ease by the cast's generous indulgence towards my 'greenness'.

We were well on into our rehearsals when disaster struck, in the form of one of the worst flu epidemics to have hit Sheffield in recent times. Every member of the cast went down with it, so it had to be cancelled. All four of my colleagues had to take to their beds. I was the only one around who was unaffected. I was probably resistant to it, having recently had a bout of flu just before coming to Sheffield.

With Chris, being physically frail, it developed into pneumonia and on the Winter Solstice, December 21st, he died. One of the last things he did a few days previously, was to get out of bed to look through his new telescope which had just arrived. He was a keen star gazer and was very excited about the new possibilities offered by it. I vividly remember the sheer delight despite his illness, of peering through it at the mountains on the moon. That was to be his last view of the heavens from earth.

His death was a devastating blow to all who were connected with the Centre, particularly of course his beloved wife, May and brother and sister-in-law. All of them were themselves severely affected by the flu. With Norman, it was particularly debilitating. His asthma got worse and he was confined to his house for weeks, and never fully recovered. That Christmas was the most sombre that I had ever experienced. A lot fell on me to comfort and console and also carry out all the practical tasks that needed to be done. So much of their work had depended on Chris' guidance. Despite his physical frailty, he had had a great reservoir of inner strength to draw on – a fine spiritual sensibility and resourcefulness of will. He was only forty-five, at the height of his powers.

For eighteen and a half years (a 'moon node', the significance of which will be explained in the last chapter on patterns and rhythms in biography and in Endnote 2) , he was responsible for continuing the work of Arnold Freeman, beginning as a twenty-five year-old at the Sheffield Educational Settlement, and then seven years later, founding Tintagel House. Another seven years were to pass before he was able to replace The Little Theatre, as it was called at the Settlement. It was only to be three years that he was able to enjoy the fruits of his labours. Learning about what all four of them went through in seeing the building project realised, it felt like a loving sacrifice of all their energy and life-forces, and in Chris' case, his personal wealth as well. Their sheer exhaustion must have made them particularly vulnerable to illness.

The funeral service was taken by the local Christian Community priest a few days after Christmas. It happened to be on the same day as the wedding of an old friend from Emerson days, Catherine, which I was invited to. For both of us, it betokened a huge change in our lives. One memory of the funeral has vividly stood out for me ever since, and that was the exact mirroring-by chance-of the shape of the coffin by the rafters of the Arnold Freeman Hall roof directly above it. (This Hall is a lovely, light-filled, many-sided room above the Theatre auditorium).

The next day I was asked to take on his work, which would basically involve directing plays, giving introductory courses on Anthroposophy to the general public and planning the cultural programme. I knew I didn't have Chris' talents, so I felt quite overwhelmed by the task ahead. But the trust and confidence they showed in me was a sustaining fount of strength for the months and years to come. Looking back to that time, it seems that the gods were saying to me, *We have given you the tools, - now get on with the job.*

From now on my life was so bound up with the life of Tintagel House and the Merlin Theatre that it would require another book to narrate all that happened, - the encounters with all the different sorts of people that came through the Centre; the successes and failures of various projects; the ordeals of the spirit we had to go through. So I will end my life story here. I doubt I will write a part 2, because the time it takes to write about one's life leaves little time to live it! And, God willing, I still have a lot of living and learning to do!

* * * * * * *

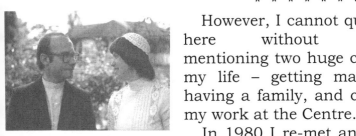

However, I cannot quite end it here without naturally mentioning two huge changes in my life – getting married and having a family, and completing my work at the Centre.

In 1980 I re-met and married Judith, having last met her twelve years previously. Without her loving support and practical good sense and also her ability of getting on with all sorts of people, I could not have managed the responsibility of running the Centre all those years. For twelve years she ran a flourishing Steiner kindergarten, not only drawing on Anthroposophical insights into the nature of young children but also on her own nursery nurse training and experience. We were blessed with two children, Hannah, and Matthew.

Both of them are now married, - Hannah to Michael, an artist and theatre scenery designer and carpenter, who used to do voluntary work at the Merlin; and Matthew to Joo  Youn, an urban designer from South Korea. Hannah is a class teacher at Wynstones Steiner School, and Matthew, an engineering geologist. I now have the privileged status of grandfather as both couples have recently have had their first child, Lin-Ah Ella and Samuel Jacob.

* * * * * * *

In 2005, due to diminishing funds, we handed the site on to Ruskin Mill Trust, which was opening a new college in Sheffield, named after Arnold Freeman. Their work is also based on the educational and social ideals of Anthroposophy, but directly concerned with meeting the needs of young people who have various forms of developmental disorders.

For 33 years I had been responsible for the running of Tintagel House and the Merlin Theatre. My last production under the old regime, was Goethe's *Faust,* (my third attempt!) which we were asked to take to the Goetheanum, - for me one of the highlights of my theatre work. For the next four years, Judith and I were both taken on by Freeman College. She taught in textiles as a felting tutor. I became a cultural diversity tutor, and under their auspices I continued to devise and deliver the programme of artistic and educational events, as well as directing plays – *Slugs and Angels,* a commissioned piece about the life of Ruskin, written by a friend, Richard Parry; *Hamlet,* which I now felt ready to direct (!), and three one-act plays by Yeats, the last one being his *Resurrection.* This was my very last production.

In 2009, we both retired from Freeman College but I have continued to organise the cultural programme on behalf of the Sheffield Group of the Anthroposophical Society. Judith continues with her crafts, particularly knitting, which she does professionally, and both of us sing in choirs. I have taken up the flute again and play in small amateur ensembles; do a bit of writing; pursue my studies of history and art and continue to run introductory courses on Anthroposophy (for my sins). My chief pleasure is still going for long walks in the Peak District.

I feel I have been very favoured by the Gods for placing me near a landscape which accords with my lifelong search for psychic and spiritual balance[1], - the

---

[1] Sheffield itself is balanced geographically between North and South and West and East, being exactly in the centre of England. Also in Anglo-Saxon times, it lay on the border between the kingdoms of Mercia and Northumbria. At the battle of

Dark Peak, of bleak, gritstone[1] moors contrasting with the White Peak, of sensuous limestone dales. The crystalline nature of the former has an awakening and bracing effect on the soul. It forces you to feel separate from your surroundings, while the porous nature of the latter, which is really the fossilised remains of ancient sea creatures, tends to draw you out into the landscape, giving rise to a dreamy consciousness. In walking extensively in the Peaks, I eventually found my ideal spot which I intuitively felt emanated a harmony of these two opposing 'energies'. My intuition was confirmed when I looked at a geological map of the area which showed it to be an isthmus of gritstone surrounded by limestone. And not only is there geological balance that any Feng Shui[2] practitioner would approve of, but this whole landscape is a wonderful, emblematic expression of spiritual evolution. It has within it, a stone circle marking the Winter Solstice, and the Midsummer Moonrise as it changes over a period of eighteen and a half years; remains of Bronze Age settlements, traces of Roman habitation and a hermit's cave, inside of which is a carved crucifix with buds sprouting from it, suggesting a Tree of Life. There are also 'fairy stories' connected with it, that is, folk tales of nature spirits. The main geological feature - a pair of rocky pillars, is called *Robin Hood's Stride*. There are many places in the Peak District named after Robin, a mythic figure predating the

---

Dore, now a suburb, Mercia defeated Northumbria, and England became one nation.

[1] A type of sandstone.

[2] An ancient art of geomancy that balances the energies of any given space to assure well-being and harmony for people inhabiting it.

legendary figure we're all familiar with. *Rob* or *Robin* is the same being as *Hob* or *Puck,* a midsummer sprite that various people in earlier times were aware of. Where they had their visionary experience, they named the spot after it. *Hood* simply means quality or state of being as in *sisterhood* or *Buddhahood.* I have spent many happy hours exploring this piece of God's earth in all weathers and times of the day and year, experiencing it as a being, a *Genius Loci,* whom one can only get to know over a period of time, just as it is with human beings. I have discovered a magical connection between all these historical and natural features, which I think tells the story of our evolution, - a story which people can experience as they walk from the Circle to the Cave. One day I hope to write a book about it all, with art, poetry and accompanying music.

On researching the area, I discovered from an elderly local historian that he had been good friends with a lady living in the area, May Melland[1], who had first awakened Arnold Freeman's interest in Steiner's political and economic ideas. When I visited the historian, he had just reprinted an article she had written in the thirties for a local magazine about the area, referring to Steiner's understanding of stone circles. It felt like another of those hidden connections which give a joy and significance to life.

Half-humorously, I have asked my family and friends to scatter my ashes, and place a seat there inscribed with the words, *Robert's Peak Experience*.[2] For me, this won't be the end, but another kind of beginning[3]. As Benjamin Franklin, the scientist and inventor said for his own epitaph,

The Body of B. Franklin, Printer, Like the Cover of an Old Book, Its Contents Torn Out And Stripped of its Lettering and Gilding, Lies Here Food_for Worms, But the Work shall not be Lost, For it Will as He Believed Appear Once More In a New and more Elegant Edition Revised and Corrected By the Author.

Or, as I have expressed recently in verse form, entitled

---

[1] Her sister was the first eurythmist in England.

[2] If you need this little joke explained, the phrase *Peak Experience* was used by the psychologist, Abram Maslow to designate a *'heightened or transcendent experience'*.

[2] For many of my Christian friends, it is hard, if not impossible, to reconcile their faith with the idea of reincarnation and karma. Please see **Endnote 7** for a justification.

.

Plant and Soul

The plant rises up to the light
From out of its seed in the soil
The soul descends to the Earth
From out of its seed in the Light.

And after their season of growth
The plant falls back to the Earth
While the soul rises up to the light.

But unlike the life-cycle of plants
With their continual repeating of type,
The rhythm of the human soul
Is in a constant process of change,
A continual metamorphosis.

In the play of life and death
The soul rehearses its part,
By ascending each night
To the source of the light
And descending to the dark of the day.

But now there is another Source
To be found streaming out of the earth.
The Light that is found in the night
Is now to be found in the day.

* * * * * * *

Before finally finishing this chapter, I would just like to
add a few remarks about how I see Anthroposophy now
after forty or so years. Its challenge as always, is how to

live it from the heart, and to regard it as an aid to acquiring fresh insights into the continually changing world we live in, rather than as a static body of knowledge. As its originator said, *My greatest task is to kindle a flame in every heart so that one can become what one really is.* Also, I have seen over the years how important it is to be aware of the enormous shift of consciousness in many different fields that has taken place over the last few decades, and to see Steiner's work as part of that greater whole.

However, it is still a wonder that it continues to be relatively unknown, at least in this country, despite its successful applications in various fields of activity such as ecological agriculture, education and social banking. To my knowledge there is no other contemporary world view that connects up what has been kept apart in our culture, such as spirituality, science and social and economic life, and at the same time, basing it on a sound epistemological and philosophical footing.

Schopenhauer said,

> *All truth passes through three stages.*
> *First it is ridiculed*
> *Second it is violently opposed.*
> *Third, it is accepted as being self-evident.*

I would say there are four stages.
First it is ignored (consciously or unconsciously)
Second it is ridiculed, etc

Biographical patterns and rhythms

Is one's life a succession of accidental happenings, interspersed with some, perhaps very few events, brought about consciously? The only shape it has, is what one imposes on it. Is it, as Macbeth cried out ...a *tale told by an idiot, full of sound and fury, signifying nothing.*? Or is it, as some religious people might say, ordained by God (or less benign agencies!)? For me, it makes sense to think that our biographical development follows certain laws, *if we have the eyes to see it,* just as there are biological and physical laws. As I have already said in the preface:- I have coined the word, *autobiosophy,* to describe what I am attempting here, - to sense the underlying wisdom (*sophia)* that guides one's life, compared with the recording of it *(graphy).* Of course, given the enormously complex phenomenon that is our life, these laws and patterns are far harder to discern. One has to remember that they are archetypes. In reality they manifest in a variety of approximate ways, with many individual variations. The question is, *What sort of hypotheses can one hold that enables us to 'read the text' that is our life and make sense of it?* Mostly it appears as a morass of squiggly lines as a book does to an illiterate person. Learning the language of biography can be an extraordinarily enriching experience. Things which at the time seemed senseless, are come to be seen years later as a meaningful part of a larger whole. Of course there can be all sorts of pitfalls, - seeing 'significance' where there is none; 'shoehorning' the facts to fit in with one's theories. However, bearing that in mind, I do think that it is possible to discern underlying patterns to one's life, and that overall it has meaning and purpose. One way of thinking about it is to see it as a work of art in the making, like a symphony or a play. Or, more specifically, perhaps one could relate it to the sonata form in music – an initial statement or theme which then gets developed, goes through all kinds of variations before finally getting restated or recapitulated but in a changed form. Although it may move through different keys, nevertheless there is one dominant key which gives it its unique character. Or one can use the analogy of a jazz composition which has a basic tune and chord structure within which free and spontaneous improvisation takes place.

We are the composer or author but one can have the very strong experience that the 'we' is very different from the 'we' we think we are! As has been indicated earlier, it is our 'higher self', the Divine within us, which shapes the necessary laws of destiny that we have to follow. Necessity is not the opposite of freedom but the 'soil' in which it can grow.

Before writing this book, I was aware of certain patterns and rhythms that I gleaned from my studies of Anthroposophy and traditional wisdom. Others emerged while writing it. I felt as if I was *seeing* them, not thinking them out. When it came to deciding how to divide my story into different chapters, it soon became clear that it naturally fell into a descending sequence of phases of a darkening consciousness - a mirroring on a microcosmic level what the Ancients described as Ages or Yugas. I am sure many people can observe the same phenomena in their own life. Wordsworth describes it in his *Ode on the Intimations of Immortality.* Here is an excerpt:-

> *Heaven lies about us in our infancy!*
> *Shades of the prison-house begin to close*
> *Upon the growing Boy,*
> *But He beholds the light, and whence it flows,*
> *He sees it in his joy;*
> *The Youth, who daily farther from the east*
> *Must travel, still is Nature's Priest,*
> *And by the vision splendid*
> *Is on his way attended;*
> *At length the Man perceives it die away,*
> *And fade into the light of common day.*

The Hindus believe that mankind has descended into lower stages of consciousness. So did the ancient Greeks. They called them the Golden Age *(Satya Yuga);* the Silver Age *(Treta Yuga);* the Bronze and Heroic Ages *(Dvapara Yuga);* and the Iron Age *(Kali Yuga).* Steiner confirms out of his own spiritual researches that they were not fanciful myths (in the conventional sense) but a true depiction of humanity gradually acquiring an earthbound consciousness and losing a spiritual one. He also added his own discovery that the Kali Yuga (which means the Age of Darkness) came to an end in 1899 AD, and a New Age of Light has now begun.

I would like now to explore in detail some of the rhythms and patterns that I am familiar with and relate them to my own life as I go along. They criss-cross the course of one's life, and weave a 'fabric' of meaning. I will begin with the 7-year biographical phases,[1] (which trace a descent, and *potential* ascent of consciousness similar to that described above. We already have names for some of those passages in life, such as infancy, childhood, adolescence, adulthood at 21 and old age.[2] Then in the Sixties the phenomenon of the mid-life crisis began to be explored. In Anthroposophical psychology there is the notion that approximately every seven years we cross a kind of threshold into another state of mind and soul. They are like a series of mini-deaths and mini-births of the psyche, where something of our past is sloughed off and new possibilities or challenges arise. For some, these transitions can be quite traumatic; for others they remain unnoticed in the unconscious. Here is a diagram that illustrates this evolutionary process.

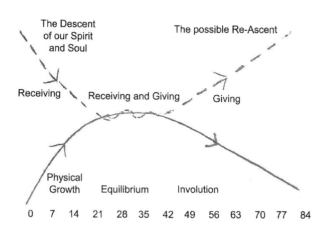

---

[1] See Professor Bernard Lievegoed's book, *Phases* which describes them in detail.
[2] Shakespeare gives his version of the Seven Ages of Man in *As You Like It.*

As you can see, we grow *up* physically, but grow *down* psychologically and spiritually. To use religious language, we take 21 years to 'incarnate' into our physical body; another 21 years to fully permeate our soul, and the time after that to discover our essential Self, the spiritual core of our being. The first 3 times 7 phase can be characterised as one where we receive from the world, through our education; the second one where we are involved in a process of both giving and receiving; and the third we can gradually become conscious of the need to give back to the world what we received from it. But that requires a change of heart and mind at a time when old certainties in our life are often beginning to crumble.

I don't remember anything significant happening around **7.** (**In my 9th year**, when I moved to a new house and school, I do remember feeling more separate from my surroundings, manifesting, as I have already recounted in chapter 2, in the desire to record my life in the way of writing a diary and taking photos. Also, I began to have intense feelings about what I saw as injustice. *(It's not fair!)*. The 9th year is a well-known rubicon, characterised as a prefiguring of adolescence – feelings of loneliness and rebelliousness against the world.)

From **14 to 21,** the young person is trying to find him or herself, amid a turmoil of newly awakened forces of sexuality as well as moral idealism. Now an independent soul life of thoughts, feelings and will-impulses begins to develop, while still being closely tied to the family. In my case this phase was particularly heightened by the death of my father and moving to a much larger school.

At 21, the traditional coming of age, the true individual identity, the Ego (Latin for *'I am'*) is beginning to manifest. The next seven years is a time when young people feel the urge to explore the world physically or mentally. If this desire is repressed by parental or social expectations generally, as it often is, then it can erupt destructively much later on in life. When I was working with young unemployed graduates in the theatre in the Eighties, I often used to reassure them that they didn't need to feel guilty, which they often did, about not having a regular job. As long as they were still learning from life in some way, it was a good time to experiment with different ways of thinking and living. If by the age of 28 or 29, they were still in that 'wandering' state, then there might well be a legitimate cause for concern!

Towards the end of my 21st year, I left university, which was a huge change in my life. Now I was really on my own, and for me the next 7 years was certainly an archetypal period of exploration of what my primary task in life should be.

At around 28, the *sentient or feeling soul* period as Steiner calls it), gives way to the *rational or mind soul*. This manifests as an urge to 'settle down', to order one's life more, commit to responsibilities at work and home. The powers of thought are used to bring about goals that you or others set. The mind now begins to feel the need for reason and consistency in the conduct of life, in contrast to responding to the whims and desires of the sentient soul.

In the middle of my 28th year, when I was in Germany, I distinctly remember feeling I wanted to end my studies and begin my life work, if only I could find it. And this was to happen at the beginning of my 29th year.

In the Middle Ages, there was a similar understanding that young people needed to go through three stages of development, specifically in those times relating to craftsmen. During the apprenticeship years from 14 to 21, the young person had to live in another craftsman's household, and learn through observation and practice. Translated into today's terms, it is often good for a teenager to live with another family, and experience how they live, particularly if they are experiencing difficulties at home, which can often be rather emotionally stifling for them. At the ages of 21, the apprentice became a journeyman and travelled round Europe, learning from different master craftsmen. And then at 28, he came back to his home country, and became a master, setting up his own workshop.

Although my life story finishes here, it might be of interest to get a glimpse of future stages of development. At **35,** a new phase begins. The *consciousness soul* is born. In this phase of life we begin to feel more self-aware, and more as a detached observer of life. In contrast to the previous period, when we were immersed in the ongoing flow of things, confidently pursuing our goals, - we now begin to experience doubt in our capabilities. This may only emerge towards the end of the thirties. Hamlet is the embodiment of this state of soul, with its inability to carry out resolutions. Goethe also characterises it in *Faust* in his figure *Sorge,* which can be translated *Care* (in the sense of *Worry* or *Anxiety).*

Come or go? Or in, or out? His resolve is lost in doubt. Midway on the beaten trail He will grope and fail; Ever straying, ever thwarted, he beholds a world distorted, Burdens others with his yoke, Grasps for breath, and then will choke...

At 35, I was directing my first production of Goethe's *Faust,* and because there was no one suitable to take on the part of Faust, I decided to do that as well. This 'Faustian' (or foolhardy) act stretched me to the limit. It was to be some years later however before the typical symptoms of the consciousness soul began to emerge. Like many people, this existential 'midlife' crisis only hits them in the forties or even later. Paradoxically, it can be a positive turning-point in one's life. Either one goes the way of the body with its declining forces (as indicated in the above diagram), following the psychological laws of inertia, - passively pursuing pleasure of various kinds – or, one begins to take up new interests, or/and develop an inner life consciously through meditation or prayer. This is now a *conscious* transformation of our thoughts, feelings and actions, leading eventually to the birth of a new faculty, called *Spirit Self (*or *Manas* in Sanskrit, where we get the word, *Man* or *Human* from).

Because we have not reached that stage in the evolution of humanity, the phases after **42** when conscious spiritual transformations are able to take place, are only in potential seed form.

Perhaps a few words need to be said here about how our individual soul development is a microcosmic recapitulation of what is writ large in the successive epochs of human history, - which is a story of unfolding soul capacities. To me this only makes sense if we think we have the opportunity to develop them in our successive lifetimes. We are now living in the *consciousness soul* period, which began in England with the development of science from the 15th century onwards, but which has now spread throughout the industrialised world. This new faculty of coolly observing the world at the exclusion of any moral or aesthetic feelings, which is the hallmark of the scientific method, has led on the one hand to an extraordinary mastery of external Nature, but on the other hand to an impoverishment of our inner life. This is a necessary stage that both the individual and humanity have to go through in order to acquire the capacity for independent judgement, free from social or religious constraints. However if we remain in this state, we are in danger of losing any deep connection with our fellow human beings and with the world of Nature, which is what is happening now. The way forward is not to reject science but to extend its parameters, so through inner development, we can develop a way of knowing which is also empathetic, - 'a thinking with the heart'. This new faculty will fully develop in the 3rd millennium, beginning with the Slav peoples.[1]

The previous cultural period is called the Graeco-Roman era (which includes the Middle Ages). This was the time of the *rational or mind soul* when the faculty of thinking was awakened and elaborated. Before that was the Egyptian and Mesopotamian cultural era of the

---

[1] In the 'mystery' language of the *Book of Revelation* this period is called *Philadelphia,* the city of brotherly love. The communist experiment in Soviet Russia was a caricatured prefiguring of this.

sentient soul, when truths were primarily inspired, rather than thought out intellectually, and expressed through myths and symbols. These large time periods last around 2000 years.[1]

Another archetypal rhythm which seems to match my actual experience is the 'lunar standstill' rhythm of **18.6 years or roughly 18 years 7 months.**[2] Many Bronze Age sites are aligned to this phenomenon, like the one in Derbyshire I mentioned earlier. Spiritually, in the life of an individual, at this age of around 18 and a half years, (and multiples thereof) there is a kind of 'opening' within the laws of one's karma which allows fresh creative forces to pour in. In my case it was a time of joy and new hope. I got offered a place at university exactly coinciding with this rhythm. On the second round, just before 37, I got married, and just after, we learnt we were to have our first child.

The next rhythm which seems to be in accord with my life is the **Saturn return of 29 and a half years.** (That is the time it takes to go round the Sun). Astrologers describe it as a time of taking up responsibility for one's life, giving it some order and structure, which is the chief influence that Saturn or Kronos brings. This was dramatically true in my case, when at the age of 29 years five months, I was asked to take on a major share of responsibility of running the Centre. Another 29 to 30 years later, beginning with the world tragedy of 9/11 which happened on my birthday, 11th September, 2001, I was embarking on what was to be my last production,-

---

[1] See **Endnote 2** for an explanation of these soul periods.
[2] See **Endnote 6**

my third attempt at Goethe's *Faust*,- before the Centre was taken over by Freeman College. It was an extraordinary year of highs and lows –increasing worries about how our small charity could go on financing our work, contrasting with the extremely positive reception our production received at the Goetheanum[1] in Switzerland. It couldn't have been a better *swansong*.

A cosmic rhythm based on the life of Christ is the one of **33 and a third years**, which is to do with death and resurrection. This is a cycle of endings and new beginnings that plays out in the life of individuals and in society.[2] In my case, when I was 33, I directed my first really successful production, which was a dramatization I made of *The Little Prince* by St Exupéry. This I felt to be the real beginning of my theatre work. At twice that age, I retired.

And then there is the biblical rhythm of **three score years and ten,** (a moon rhythm of 7x10) which I have experienced this year (2013-2014). Halfway is the turning-point of 35, the deepest point of incarnation, which I have described above.

And finally the sun rhythm of **72 years** (12x6) which traditionally is regarded as our natural life span. Although today it has been considerably extended due to

---

[1] It was like taking coals to Newcastle. They regularly put on productions of the original, but I think ours was one of the first in English translation, which greatly pleased the mostly American audience. (It was part of an international conference in English).

[2] A *centenary* is particularly significant which is 3 times 33 and a third years. At the time of writing, spring 2014, the troubles in Ukraine are an echo of the outbreak of the 1st World War.

advances in medicine and hygiene, it can feel like a kind of blessing to have passed that threshold. Freed from the constraints of the workings of destiny, it can become a time of grace; a time of increased creativity, as shown in the lives of many artists, musicians and writers, such as Grandma Moses, Hokusai, Sibelius, Verdi and Goethe.[1]

* * * * * * *

The objection may be made, *Would we necessarily lead better lives, knowing about all these different rhythms I have described in this chapter?* No, not necessarily, but expanding our imaginative awareness of such phenomena can help us to have a more objective and accepting attitude to what is going on in our and other people's lives, either when we are in the midst of them, or afterwards when we look back.

Another objection could also be made that the rich fabric of life with all its mysteries can't be so prosaically explained away. I would argue that paradoxically, the sense of mystery and wonder increases, the more we understand the extraordinary structures that underlie the course of our life, just as it does when studying any natural phenomenon. It's a never-ending quest of understanding.

* * * * * *

---

[1] Please see **Endnote 6** for a full description of how we are embedded as microcosm in the macrocosm through these sun and moon rhythms. It is taken from Steiner's set of lectures, entitled *'Man, Hieroglyph of the Universe'* which he gave in 1920.

I would like now to share with the reader a curious pattern of recapitulations or 'echoes' that I have noticed in a particular time of my life described in this book. There may be more, but these stand out quite prominently. I don't know what particular significance they may have, (if any!). (*I would be interested to hear from anyone who has had similar odd experiences, or indeed generally about any rhythms they may have noticed in their life. My email address is at the back of the book*).

Because I have described these particular events and experiences in detail earlier in the book but without making the connections between all of them, I will here systematically point out what I think are recapitulations of the earlier events, but which are now at a quicker rate. They are not repetitions exactly, but metamorphosed versions in another 'key'.

Here are the comparisons: - (in sections A and B are a series of 'idylls' between two phases).

A. 1959. Between 'O' levels and the 6th form.
B. 1966. Between a somewhat austere stay in Germany and Austria and the next phase in London, is a 'paradisal' interlude - a two week Sicilian idyll experiencing the beauties of art and nature, shared with a Jewish girl.
C. 1966. After leaving University, I go to Germany and then to

A. 1962. Between school and university.
B. 1972. Between a somewhat austere stay in Germany and the next phase in London, is a 'paradisal' interlude – a two-week idyll in Northern Italy, experiencing the beauties of art and nature, shared with a Jewish girl.
C. 1971. After leaving Emerson College, I go to Germany and

Austria, where I get to know two women who manifest diametrically opposed 'energies', - what I like to call the Dionysian and Apollonian Polarity.

experience the same polarity, but spiritually enhanced. (This experience of pairs of people who have influenced me is a constant theme in my biography. I met it again in Sheffield. May Boulton's warmth and artistic sensibility contrasted beautifully with the clarity of thought and strength of will of Marjory Battersby, another key supporter of the Centre).

D. 1966-69. I work in a language school in Central London for 3 years. The Principal has strikingly dark, intense eyes.

D. 1972. I work in a language school, this time in North London, for 3 weeks. The Principal has strikingly dark, intense eyes.

* * * * * * *

I would now like to conclude with what I think is the most significant motif in this first part of my life. I have already partly pointed out examples of it in the course of the narrative. It could be described as a progressive revelation (or uncovering) of *what I am not,* or rather, becoming conscious of *what I am,* and realising I needed to acknowledge and if possible, overcome the mental and spiritual limitations that I had just passively inherited from the age I am living in. This was a painful process of letting fall away veils of illusion that were barriers to self-knowledge. And this also meant having to learn to see through the veils that others wore, and not judge them by appearances.[1]

All this was not brought about by a conscious path of inner development, but was forced on me from without. That's why I have given the title of this book, *A Kind of Initiation*, - an initiation from life itself.

The first illusion was thinking that really we are basically all the same, or rather expecting other nations to be like us, or *ought* to be like us. Living in Germany and Austria made me acutely conscious of how thoroughly English I was, (despite being half-Austrian by birth). This realisation of how much we are influenced by our national culture gave rise to the question, **Who are we beyond these given conditions?** Our national identity is a garment that many of us are hardly aware that we are wearing. No true peace between nations can be realised until this is experienced.

The second 'unveiling' was of the mental and spiritual 'mindset' that we unconsciously absorb through our education and upbringing. In my case it was a 'liberal', English understanding of Christianity which uncritically accepted, or stood alongside with, the secular intellectual assumptions of what constitutes truth. As I have described in earlier chapters, it took some dramatic and almost visceral experiences to convince me that *There are more things in heaven and earth, Horatio, Than are dreamt of in your philosophy. (Hamlet).* Jesus is not just a good man but also an embodiment of a cosmic reality that has to be experienced and not just believed

---

[1] Connected with this, I recently wrote a light satirical poem directed against myself. See **Appendices 6.**

in. Evil is not just an absence of goodness, but also a cosmic reality that is not only 'out there', but also within us, for which we need to take responsibility to become aware of, and to tame and re-direct its energies. And these modern religious assumptions are embedded in a larger cultural narrative, which states that our ancestors were more ignorant than us. Now we know better. Only the realisation that what they intuitively knew in the form of myth and symbol can now be rediscovered on a conscious level, helped me to dispel that illusion.

The third discovery was the fact that we cannot be fully identified with our gender. This was less of a consciously articulated thought – more of a gradually dawning awareness in my twenties. It has been a great moral advance in our times that the feminist and gay liberation movements have helped to bring about since the sixties. I did not primarily regard my uncle as a homosexual but as a loving individual who in those fairly recent times, had to suffer greatly for something that he was born with.

It is interesting to note that that boys and girls were educated together in both the primary and secondary years in the Steiner schools that were being set up in the 1920's, a radical move in those days. Also in the Christian Community Church which was founded also in the twenties, both men and women could become priests, able to administer the sacraments.

In my brief experience in a London secondary modern school, of teaching 'working class' pupils, some of whom were West Indians, it was painfully brought home to me the realisation how middle class I was, and that I had previously had very little contact with black culture. So these were two more 'garments' that had to be discarded. Again great advances have been made in the last forty years or so in the realms of understanding social class and ethnicity.

Unfortunately now though, there is the tendency to refuse to acknowledge that there *are* real (though not final) differences between the nations, ethnic groupings and sexes, to such an extent that you cannot make jokes about them in some 'progressive' circles. This is ultimately due to a static view of the human personality which does not allow for personal growth and change. In a *dynamic* model of the human psyche, it is our 'higher self', the Spirit in us, which can transform and go beyond those provisional 'soul' manifestations of gender, nationality, ethnicity and also religion. I call it 'soul' because it is the private or subjective part of us arising from our environment and heredity.[1] The act of attempting to understand objectively how these influences of Nature and Nurture affect our inner life enables us to modify and change them. That is an activity of our Spirit. And that brings us back to what I alluded to on p.161, which was the devastating consequences of a Church Council in Constantinople in 879AD when the Spirit or 'Higher Soul' in us was proclaimed as not being a property of human nature. We are creatures of body and soul only. I doubt whether those Christians who argue against women priests, or those who claim their nation or race is superior to others, are aware of how and where their thought forms

---

[1] For me it is the same as 'personality' which literally means 'a mask' (*persona* – Latin). What can *sound through* (*per sona*) the mask is what I call 'the individuality' (that which cannot be divided). That is our spiritually unique self.

originated! Although our bodies and souls are different, in the Spirit we have equal value– both before God and before the law. (It is a paradox of course because the very nature of our spirit is that it is *uniquely* different!).

All I have tried to indicate in this last chapter is that the more we become aware of how our thoughts and feelings are influenced by all manner of things, - the particular phase of life we are passing through, or the longer-lasting effects of our heredity and cultural environment, - the more we are able to sense the presence of a hidden third element in our nature – beyond nature and nurture, beyond body and soul. This is the Wise Being within us who guides our destiny. It is the mysterious entity whose name can only be applied to itself – the 'I', that is, the doorway to a higher realm.

Let a poem, a picture[1] and St. John's Gospel[2] have the last say.[3]

"I Am Not I" by Juan Ramon Jimenez.

Translated by Robert Bly

I am not I.
I am this one
walking beside me whom I do not see,
whom at times I manage to visit,
and whom at other times I forget;
who remains calm and silent while I talk,
and forgives, gently, when I hate,

---

[1] I owe this picture to Russell Evans
[2] Ch 10, v 9
[3] Not quite! A simple verse came into my mind while writing about this. See **Appendices 7.**

who walks where I am not,
who will remain standing when I die.

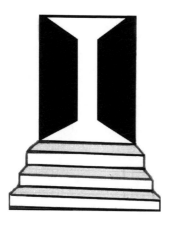

I am the Door

AFTERWORD

I would like say a few words about my siblings' subsequent lives.

Olga got married to Ted, a probation officer, and they had three children, a boy and two girls, all of whom were educated at Wynstones, their local Steiner school. She continued with her nursing and became a strong supporter of the school and the local Christian Community Church. They now have nine grandchildren. Her openheartedness has won her lots of friends.

John left school at 16 and after a few labouring jobs enrolled on a building course at the local technical college. He had at last found out what he wanted to do. After college, he joined a building company, and eventually worked his way up to becoming a director. His wife, Sheila and he were childhood sweethearts with the same birthday, but a year apart. They had a girl, and then a boy. They now have three grandchildren. All his life has been a courageous battle against ill health, which has forged a strong and forthright spirit.

James married an Austrian girl, Christl, (he had a penchant for foreign young ladies as I remember!) and they soon had a girl and then a boy. Like John, he didn't want to stay on at school and left to become an architectural assistant in a local architect's firm as he was good at design. He studied at night school and eventually worked himself up to becoming a co-director of a medium-sized architectural practice without having fully completed his training. They now have five grandchildren. His innate optimism and cheerfulness of spirit has sustained him through various trials.

Otto, the classic rebellious second born, was the 'black sheep' of the family. He hated school and left at fifteen. In desperation, my father on the advice of a friend sent him to another school in Gloucestershire which 'was able to deal with difficult youngsters'. This turned out to be Wynstones School - the only connection with the Steiner movement the family had, until I discovered it independently nearly 20 years later. And now my daughter Hannah is working there as a class teacher.

Although he remembers it fondly, he was eager to get out into the real world and left after a year. Through family connections he eventually ended up as a farm labourer in Wales. He had found his vocation. After a few years he became a shepherd in the Cotswolds, and then a farm manager, working for the only Communist Lord in the House of Lords, Lord Wogan Philips. (His maiden speech was to advocate abolishing it!) Around this time he met his future wife, Eileen, and like the others immediately started a family, which grew to five – three boys and two girls. They moved to Suffolk where he became a farming instructor for a Borstal institution, as I mentioned earlier. They had eleven grandchildren. He died recently in 2013. He had an unerring sense for goodness, as well as a wonderful sense of humour.

David followed in his father's footsteps, and was the typical dutiful and conscientious first-born. He worked hard and was good at everything at school. Then followed two years national service, which he said was good for his character development. After a spell as an interpreter for the Intelligence Services in Vienna (this was not long after the War), he enrolled in his father's old college – Fitzwilliam House, Cambridge to study French and German. After graduating, he trained to become an Anglican priest. After two curacies in Brighouse and Sheffield, he followed the call to becoming an Anglican monk of the Community of the Resurrection, a relatively open order whose main work was teaching and social work. He left after thirty years to marry. He died in the same month as Otto. His great virtues were constancy and steadfastness of purpose.

It is to them, my parents, my wife and family and all the others, who knowingly or unknowingly have helped me along the labyrinthine paths of my life, that I dedicate this book.

Endnotes

1. Reflecting years later, on what I had experienced of the way philosophy was taught then and I believe still is,[1] I thought a much more fruitful and meaningful way would be to begin with the students' own experiences, not only in relation to ethical questions, but also to *how* they actually perceive and think about things. This would demand a much more experiential way of attending to the more subtle aspects of thought and perception. Instead of playing an intellectual game of refutation and counter-refutation of speculative ideas, the role of philosophy should now be to really explore its key activity itself, that is, the processes of thinking and perception, above all, the former, as it is only through thinking that you can arrive at a basis of any statements and propositions about oneself and the world. It is interesting that in the U.S. neuroscientists and meditators are collaborating together to try and understand the workings of the mind. Why couldn't philosophers join in that collaboration? Or perhaps they do, but not I think in this country, but I may be wrong. Then philosophy could contribute to extending our knowledge of the world, instead of being a highly specialised and arcane pursuit which is not seen as being relevant to our existence as human beings.

I could envisage a new kind of *university* (not the '*multi*versity' we have now) which would demand that *all*

---

[1] I have just been told of a university course in philosophy where the emphasis is on doing it, rather than learning about it.

students, whatever subject they are studying, from veterinary science to law, would spend a term or two at the beginning of their course, exploring how they habitually think and perceive, - a kind of experiential phenomenological epistemology! What fascinating conversations one could have across the disciplines! No previous knowledge or experience would be required – just a willingness to listen to different points of view and to examine one's own presuppositions about life. (One could imagine the architecture to be such that students from different disciplines would be encouraged to commingle in common spaces where it would be natural for them to meet and talk). Those specialising in philosophy itself would then take it further, but for the first year at least, would <u>not</u> be encouraged to *read* any philosophy, whether primary or secondary sources! Only after a spell of *doing* philosophy, no matter in how naïve and unsophisticated a way, would one then be ready to study the great thinkers. Also I think it would be necessary to practise the arts, - painting, singing, dancing etc. - alongside all the mental activity, not only as providing a therapeutic balance, but also as a way of training the student's perceptual skills which would help in the observation of their states of mind. For example, the honing of one's listening skills which would arise from working with music or speech would benefit students of law and medicine, - perhaps not physics and engineering directly (!) but could do so in relation to the fact they have to work with colleagues. As for students of philosophy and psychology, it would provide research material for theories of perception!

Could one dare suggest that also the student should do some manual craft - gardening, metalwork etc., not only as another counter balance to all the head work but also to connect up more neural pathways that current research is now showing to be the case. So being more intelligent with one's hand, eye or ear (7 kinds of intelligences have now been recognised) can only be a beneficial addition to the traditional skills of thinking. Again it could serve as research material – *how* one thinks after different forms of physical exercise.

So let's put back the *universal* into *university* where now two mathematicians can't understand each other, let alone a physicist and a theologian, and provide the opportunity of experiencing a glimpse, if nothing more, of the essential *unity* of human knowledge, 'a turning into one' as the word *'universe'* literally means.

Theology used to be regarded as the Queen of the Sciences in the Middle Ages. Now perhaps it is the turn after four hundred years of increasing specialisation where we know more and more about less and less, of Philosophy, or more particularly, Epistemology as being the new Queen of Wisdom who should reign in our universities, After all, does not 'philosophy' literally mean *'love (philo) of wisdom (Sophia)'*? Is this all a pipe dream? I think not, but it may take another hundred years before the whole system of acquiring and conveying knowledge breaks down and people will be open to new possibilities. After all, did it not take three hundred years before the sciences were regarded as disciplines in their own right, rather than handmaidens to what was called 'natural philosophy'? So perhaps the wheel can turn again!

2. The cultural period of 2160 years.

This is the time it takes the Sun to pass through one sign of the Zodiac, that is, when the Sun rises at the Spring Equinox under a different sign. It is a twelfth of the whole cycle of the Platonic Year – 25,920 years. *See Endnote 6.*

According to Steiner's seership, spiritual influences that emanate from a particular constellation, change when the Sun moves into a different one every 2176 years. During this time, the whole cultural climate on Earth changes. For our spiritual and mental development, we need to incarnate twice in this period, once as a man and once as a woman, to experience those particular conditions. However that is a tendency, not an iron law. The exceptional times we live in today means there are more frequent incarnations (of which there are many reports).

We are still living in the age of Pisces but moving into Aquarius some centuries hence. The previous period was the age of Aries (Ram). (Christ was symbolised as both a lamb and a fish). The Golden Fleece legend marks the transition from the previous epoch, the Age of Taurus, to Aries. The Bull Culture is the emblem of what Steiner calls the Egypto-Chaldean epoch, ending with Theseus slaying of the Minotaur (the half-bull man) in Crete. The bull symbol signifies the old clairvoyant forces. Theseus goes on to found Athens as a centre of the new epoch in which rational thinking begins to develop. The previous epoch to Taurus is the Ancient Persian one, whose emblem is Gemini (the Twins). Its sign **II** means dualism, expressing the opposition between the forces of Good and Evil, which is the hallmark of Zoroastrianism.

The period before that was the Ancient Indian one, which was under Cancer. Its sign ♋ shows the ending of a larger cycle of time periods, which Steiner calls the Atlantean one, and the beginning of another which he calls the Post-Atlantean one, of which there are seven smaller periods of 2000+ years each. We are in the Fifth.

3. Anthroposophical medicine grew out of the collaborative work of Steiner with a Dutch doctor, Ita Wegman. They regarded it as an extended form of medicine, adding to the discoveries of existing alleopathic methods. That is, they recognised the achievements of conventional medicine but saw the necessity of developing deeper and more long-lasting methods of healing, which took into account the reality of the psyche and our inner core, - our spiritual identity. The training is long and arduous, on top of a regular medical training, and goes on throughout a doctor's life. There are only a few in England, but hundreds in Italy and Brazil.

4. The Arthurian community of twelve 'knights' signify the necessity of twelve points of view, all equally valid, but by themselves, one-sided. The figure of Arthur ('Arcturus') moves through all of them, like the sun through the signs of the Zodiac, just as Anthroposophy is not the thirteenth point of view, but the *ability* to understand and relate to all the other twelve. Also was explained the Arthurian, Celtic stream of Christianity, which Steiner describes in his book, *Cosmic Christianity* after his visit to Tintagel in Cornwall in 1922. The word *Arthur* denotes a particular level of spiritual attainment, like the word *Buddha'* Just as there is more than one Buddha, so there have been many 'Arthurs'. That explains why there are different parts of the country associated with Arthur. The Cornish pre-Christian Arthur was a clairvoyant initiate who perceived the descent of the Christ revealed through Nature's elements.

5. The Spirit of the Age.

It is an ancient esoteric teaching that Johannes Trithemius, Abbot of Sponheim (1462-1516) promulgated, - confirmed by Steiner and most recently elaborated upon by Emil Pales, a research fellow in the Slovak Academy of Sciences, - that there are smaller shifts of consciousness every 300 or so years (a seventh of the larger period of 2160 years). These are ruled over by the seven Archangels who in turn become an Archai, the Spirit of the Age.

6. An excerpt from *Man as Hieroglyph of the Universe* by Steiner (*translated by George and Mary Adams*).

We shall now have to consider a correspondence that is found to exist in respect of Number...In his rhythm of breathing, 18 per minute- Man manifests something which is in remarkable accord with other processes of the Universe. We make 18 breaths a minute, which gives when calculated for the day, 25,920 breaths. And we arrive at the same time when we calculate how many days are contained in the traditional life span of 72 years. That also gives about 25,920 days; so that something may be said to exhale our astral body and Ego (that is, our soul and Spirit), on falling asleep and inhale them again upon waking – always in accord with the same number rhythm.

And again, when we consider how the Sun moves-whether apparently or really, does not matter – advancing a little each year in what we call the precession of the equinoxes, when we consider the number of years it takes the Sun to make this journey round the whole Zodiac, once more we get 25,920 years – the Platonic Year.

The fact is, this human life of ours, within the boundaries set by birth and death, is indeed fashioned, down to its most infinitesimal processes – as we have seen in the breathing – in accordance with the laws of the Universe.... There are other very important correspondences. For example, consider the following: - I want to lead you through Number to something else I have to bring before you. Take the 18 breaths a minute, making 1080 per hour and in 24 hours 25,920 breaths; that is we must multiply: 18x60x24 to arrive at 25,920.

Taking this as the cycle of the precession of the equinoxes, and dividing it by 60 and again by 24, we would naturally get 18 years. And what do these 18 years really mean?

Consider – these 25,920 breaths correspond to a human day of 24 hours; in other words, this 24 hour day is the day of the Microcosm. 18 breaths may serve as the unit of rhythm.

And now take the complete circle described by the precession of the equinoxes, and call it, not a Platonic Year, but a great Day of the Heavens, a Macrocosmic day. How long would one breath on this scale have to occupy to correspond with the human respiration? Its duration would have to be 18 years – a breath made by the being corresponding to the macrocosm.

Now take that which the astronomer of today calls the Nutation of the Earth's Axis. You are aware that it lies obliquely upon the Ecliptic, and the astronomers speak of an oscillation of the earth's axis around this point and they call this 'Nutation'. The axis completes one revolution around this point in just about 18 years (it is really 18 years, 7 months, but we need not consider this fraction, although it is quite possible to calculate this too with exactitude.) But with these 18 years something else is intimately connected. For it is not merely on the fact of Nutation – this 'trembling', this rotation of the Earth's axis in a double cone around the Earth's centre, and the period of 18 years for its completion – it is not only on this fact that we have to fix our minds, but we find that simultaneously with it another process takes place. The Moon appears each year in a different position because, like the Sun, she ascends and descends from the ecliptic, proceeding in a kind of oscillating motion again and again towards the Equator ecliptic. And every 18 years she appears once more in the same position she occupied 18 years before. You see that there is a connection between this Nutation and the path of the moon. Nutation in truth indicates nothing else than the moon's path. So that we can in actual reality observe the 'breathing' of the Macrocosm. .... The

Earth dances, and she dances in such a manner as to describe a cone, a double cone, in 18 years, and this dancing is a reflection of the macrocosmic breathing. This takes place just as many times in the macrocosmic year as the18 human breaths during the microcosmic day of 24 hours.

So we really have one macrocosmic breath per minute in this nutation movement. In other words, we look into this breathing of the macrocosm through this Nutation movement of the Moon, and we have before us what corresponds to respiration in man. And now what is the purport of all this? The meaning of it is that as we pass from waking to sleep, or only from the wholly conscious to the dream state, we enter another world, and over against the ordinary laws of days, years, etc., and also the Platonic Year, we find in this insertion of a moon rhythm, something that has the same relationship in the macrocosm, as breathing, the semi-conscious process of respiration, has to our full consciousness. We have therefore not only to consider a world which is spread out before us, but another world which projects into, and permeates our own.....

There can therefore be no question of having only one world in our environment. We have that world that we can follow as the world of the senses; but then we have a world, whose foundations are laid within the laws of another, and which stands in exactly the same relationship to the world of the senses, as our breathing does to our consciousness; and this other world is revealed to us as soon as we interpret in the right way this Moon movement, this Nutation of the Earth's axis....

And now, you see, these are the things in which the spiritual and material (so-called) touch each other, or let us say the psychical and material. He who can faithfully observe what is contained within his own self will find the following. These things must gradually be brought to the attention of humanity... Few can notice as yet, not having been trained to do so, the effects and important changes taking place within the individual soul at these 18.6 year periods. The nights passed through these times are the most important nights in the life of the individual. It is here where the macrocosm completes its 18 respirations, completes one minute – and Man as it were, opens a window facing quite another world... we breathe in the astral (soul) world (my summary)....

Now a certain astronomical fact was observed even in the most ancient times. Many thousands of years before the Christian era, the Egyptians knew that after a period of 72 years the fixed stars in their apparent course gain one day on the Sun. it seems to us, does it not, that the fixed stars revolve and the Sun too revolves, but that the latter revolves more slowly, so that after 72 years the stars are appreciably ahead. This the reason of the movement of the Vernal Point (the Spring Equinoctial point); namely, that the stars go faster. The Spring Equinox moves further and further away, the fixed star has altered its place in relation to the Sun. Briefly, the facts are that if we notice the path of a fixed star and notice the point where the Sun stands over it, we find that at the end of 72 years the star occupies the same position on the 30th December, while the Sun only reaches that point again on the 31st December. The Sun has lost a day. After a lapse of 25,920 years this loss is so great, that the sun has described a complete revolution and once again is back upon the place we noted. We see therefore in that in 72 years the Sun is one day behind the fixed stars. Now these 72 years are approximately the normal life period of man, and they are composed of 25,920 days.

Thus when we multiply 72 years by 360, and consider the human span of life as one day, we have the human life as one day of the macrocosm; **Man is breathed out, as it were, from the Macrocosm; his life is one day in the macrocosmic year....**

7. My simple reasoning is that if Christ is to be seen as our Ideal, then it would require more than one life to be anywhere like Him, (to put it mildly!) particularly if we died young or were brought up in a non-Christian culture, or if we were born before Christ came to earth. It will take many lifetimes before our true selves are able to emerge through all the temporary veils of ethnicity, religion (culturally determined), gender, class etc. To those who say, *Well, all this can take place in Heaven,* I would reply, *So what's the purpose of being on Earth? Why didn't we stay in a purely spiritual world?* I would agree with the poet, Robert Frost, who said, *Earth's the right place for love.* For it is only through the resistances that Earth provides, that we hone our capacities for being able to love out of inner freedom.

Another common objection is that *It's not in the Bible.*

My response to that is to point out that neither are the laws of gravity or the second law of thermodynamics. (Although there are quite explicit references if one has the eyes to see it. When asked, *Why then say the scribes that Elias (Elijah) must first come?* Christ replied that the scribes were right about this and that Elias had already come. It is also written that the disciples understood that he was speaking of John the Baptist. (*St. Matthew, Ch. 17, v. 10 – 13*).

Christ also said, *I have yet many things to say unto you, but you cannot bear them now.* (*St. John, Ch. 16, v 12*).

It was not an essential truth to be emphasised at that time. Humanity had to learn to concentrate on one life for a while, but now after 2000 years, we are ready to expand our spiritual and moral horizons.

For a more substantial Christian defence of reincarnation, see *The Case for Reincarnation* by the Rev. Leslie Weatherhead, a Methodist minister and theologian, and *The Scientist of the Invisible* by the Rev. A.P. Shepherd, onetime Canon of Worcester Cathedral. Karl Rahner, the eminent Catholic theologian of the 20th century, cautiously suggests it is a plausible theory, in his book, *A Basic Course in Belief.*

Appendices

1. And the Sound became Sun

On a darkening country day
From out of the slowly condensing whorl
White stalks of sound
Pierced through the mind
And flowered
Into
Stars

Light years away
The being that I was
Came back
Flared up
For a second
Glowed
And was gone

The Sun became sound again
And the flower folded back into the bud

2. Sounds at night become light

Sounds at night
Become light

When it was dark
A dog's bark
Eddied me back
In a whirlwind of black
To a sudden silver flare

Revealing the boy
Grubby-kneed
Trying hard
Not to heed
His mother crying, *Oi*
Come here!
Time for bed
And the light
Went out

3. Soul

Soul can be whole
Or a hole
Filled to the brim
Or an aching void
Soul can be seen in the eyes
And heard in the word

But when the gaze is vacant
And the speech is dull
You have to dig deep to find it
Hiding in the dark
O let it shine forth
With focussed rays of light and warmth
Only then will other souls respond
Like flowers unfolding
To the light of the Sun

4. The Spirit of Wholeness

The Holy Spirit heals the split
Between the ideal and the real.

What is symbolic unites.
What is diabolic divides.

We are living in diabolic times.
We are divided from Nature,
Our Mother, and the Heavens, our Father.
We are divided from each other.
We are divided within ourselves.

Matter is divided from mind,
And the heart is divided from the head.
Fact is divided from meaning,
And truth from virtue and beauty.

Come, Holy Spirit, and make us whole,
And help us see the world symbolically.

Matter illumined by spirit
And spirit given form by substance.

The wheat is His body
And the sap is His Blood.
The whole world is a sacrament
If you learn to see it aright.

(*I was intrigued by the fact that the words 'Symbolic' and 'Diabolic' mean the opposite in their original Greek form. The latter means 'something that is thrown apart'; the former is 'something that is drawn together'*).

5. Look, Listen

Look. Listen. Feel. Touch.
Don't rush.
Slow down.
Let the world come in.
You'll be surprised
At what the eyes
Can see,
And what the ears
Can hear.
There is no other world
But this.
Here. Now.
Facts. Things
Are icebergs
Tips of.

6. Self-Knowledge or Le Misanthrope?

I can't stand the English
And I can't stand the French
I can't stand the Germans
Not to mention the Chinese

But John is OK
And so is Jean
And also Johannes
As well as Han

I can't stand the working class
With their *Sun* and their *Sport*
Nor the middle class, smug with their *Mail*

And as for the liberal intellectuals
And the public school financiers
Well, they're just beyond the pale.

But I do like Sophy and Jemima and Mary and Dale
But let's face it,
The only one I can really stand...is Me
The one with the totally unique identity!

7. In the Spirit

In the Spirit..
I am not this, I am not that.
I am not thin, I am not fat.
I am not black, I am not white.
I am not dull, I am not bright.
I am not gay, I am not straight.
But... I am the Door, I am the Gate
Into that realm wherein lies my fate.

Epilogue - The Old Man's Dream

The old man dozes off after lunch and he has a most wondrous dream. He feels he is an eagle glinting gold in the sunlight, swooping and gliding effortlessly in the sky. A glorious feeling of harmony and lightness suffuses his whole being. The next thing he knows, - as if it is the most natural thing in the world, - he becomes a dove shining silver in the moonlight. Now he feels closer to the earth as he flies through the moon's shadows. But still he has the freedom of the sky. Then all of a sudden he finds himself turned into a bronze-coloured rooster strutting around on the earth itself. He can still fly if only for a few yards but he is much happier perched on dung heaps waking people up.

Then everything goes dark and he feels himself becoming human. Gradually he becomes aware that he is not alone. All around him emerging out of the gloom, are others who are dressed like him in dull grey garments. They are all arguing about whether there is such a thing as light, and the more they argue, the darker their clothes become. Most ridicule the notion, but there are a few who remember an old story about the time when light did exist, but they have no idea of how to imagine it. The young man though, still has vivid memories of being a bird in the sunlight, which for a time is something of a comfort in this all-encompassing darkness.

Then one day he finds himself all alone apparelled in black armour, astride a magnificent black horse. A still small voice inside him says, *You are now going on a quest for the Light and it is necessary that you will have to go through many ordeals. First, you will need to cross deserts and seas to reach the Land of the Black Ravens where you will find a castle of the same name. Request to be a guest there.* He does as his voice bids him, although strangely enough he doesn't actually hear it. He eventually finds the castle and is warmly received. Without more ado, he is shown his room which is covered all over with mirrors, even on the floor and ceiling. Everywhere he looks, he sees only himself, sometimes bright and clear, sometimes dull and cloudy, sometimes hideously distorted. Feeling quite nauseous he tries to get out of the room but it is locked. In blind rage he charges with his lance at the large bright mirror and smashes it into smithereens. He now finds himself in the open air. Then his voice whispers to him, "*Your task now is to find the Dragon. Don't worry, he's got so used to people not noticing him, he's got rather blasé about his safety*". "*Shall I kill him?*" asked the young knight. "*No, just mark the place where he is so that others will know that he's there*". "*How do I do that?*" "*You will know what to do when the time comes. Oh and one more thing. You must leave your horse behind, because as soon as the Dragon gets a whiff of it, his wrath is aroused, and that might make everything more difficult for you*".

Off the young man goes, now without his horse. For miles he trudges wearily across featureless flat plains, until he first smells and then sees sulphurous smoke belching out from a cave in the distance. He approaches cautiously and sees it lying there at the mouth of the cave. It is a huge beast with a dirty-red, leathery and cracked skin. It looks as if it is sleeping, then suddenly it opens one bloodshot eye and its tail flickers. Our young knight instinctively draws his sword, and is about to plunge it into the beast's body when he remembers he mustn't kill it but he is to mark the place where it is. So he sticks his sword into the earth instead, and hurries away. The Beast doesn't follow. *"Good"*, says the voice. *"Now travel south to a city where you will see more belching smoke but this time it is caused by men. You will be offered somewhere to stay. You are now without your horse and your sword. More will follow"*. The knight doesn't quite know what it means by *'More will follow'*, but he travels on obediently towards the Sun, as it is now high in the heavens. On the way he meets various travellers and tells them about the Dragon but no one wants to listen. Eventually he arrives at the city gates and slumps to the ground in complete exhaustion. Someone takes pity on him and offers him accommodation in his master's hall. He gladly accepts and is shown into a room. His heart sinks for everywhere there are mirrors again. He is about to ask if there is another room he can stay in when the door is quickly locked behind him. Now what is he going to do? The mirrors are different this time. Wherever he looks, he sees himself with a different shield. One has a double-headed eagle on it, another a lion rampant, another two standing lions, another, a fleur-de-lys, yet another, a deer's head and so it goes on. And then there are those with all sorts of geometrical designs in different colours. As our young knight looks round at himself he begins to hear different languages babbling out of the mirrors, softly at first, and then they get louder and louder, - so loud it nearly drives him mad. Not knowing what he is doing, he picks up his shield and flings it at the mirror which reflects his own shield, whereupon both shatter into fragments. At that moment, the door opens and the servant, enters quietly and without turning a hair, smiles and leads him into another room and locks the door behind him. Here is just one mirror and he at first refuses to look into it. However as tiredness overcomes him, he finds his eyes straying in that direction and what he sees astonishes him. His reflection slowly and continuously turns from being a male figure into a female one and back again and sometimes stops halfway for a few moments. Eventually he falls asleep, and the next morning, the servant enters and asks the young knight if he would like to meet his master. *He is ill in bed and cannot speak but he wants to see you for you know each other. Oh, and please bring your lance with you.* He is ushered into the sick room and sees lying on the bed an aged man with noble brow and piercing eyes. He is beckoned to sit down at his bedside and they look at each other for some minutes. And then the old man breaks into a smile and at once the knight recognises him as his long-lost uncle. His heart goes out to him and he wonders how he can help him. The servant reads his thoughts and says, *There's only one thing you can do to ease his pain. Leave your lance lying beside him. It was another's lance that pierced his thigh and the wound has never healed. He knew that one day his nephew would come with a lance that has not yet harmed anyone. Only such a lance lying near him will keep him alive.* The old man suddenly looks tired and beckons them to leave.

Our young knight now finds he is by himself in the open air, feeling somewhat unprotected. Not only does he not have his horse, sword, and shield, he now has to give up his lance as well. Then suddenly he remembers what his voice told him after he had to leave his sword stuck in the ground outside the Dragon's cave. *More will follow.* Now he understands what this means. He realises with horror that he might lose yet more of his armour. Then his voice speaks to him quietly, *Don't worry. Have faith. You will always be protected. As a reward for passing through all these trials, I will show you the way to the Castle of the Red Queen. There you will experience many delights,* (and he paused, smiling) *and there are no mirrors!*

He is led to a small, modest castle at the edge of the city, surrounded by black buildings belching smoke out of their tall chimneys. He knocks on the door and it is opened by a bevy of giggling children who invite him in without more ado. He is led into a large room where the Queen is holding court with many people. There is much feasting and laughter and he is invited to join them as if he is their long-lost friend. The company are keen to hear of the knight's adventures, and they tell him their tales. The conversation flows effortlessly into the small hours of the morning.

Now I know why she is called the Red Queen. I have never seen a woman with such long flaming-red hair. How merrily she converses and yet how gracious she is to everyone, solicitous to their every need. What an energy of delight she radiates out into the room!

The knight finds himself falling in love with her despite knowing she is married to the King and has three lovely children. He sighs. *I will just have to be content with serving her as a pure and noble knight,* but he doesn't quite convince himself. Then his voice says, *You must take your leave. It is late. Go back to where you were staying last night. There is another trial that you must go through.* As he departs, the Queen begs him to come again tomorrow when there will be much music and dancing.

That night or rather morning as it is after midnight, he has the most terrifying ordeal yet. All the mirrors are now distorting ones, and he sees grotesque images of himself. It is like a grisly parade of the Seven Deadly Sins. He rushes to the door to get out but it is locked again. All night his different faces leer at him. He can't get to sleep. And at sunrise, he slumps to the floor sobbing. When it subsides he hears his voice gently telling him, *You need to learn the secrets of the human heart. All that you have been taught up till now by Holy*

Mother Church must be refashioned from within. Now go and visit the Red Queen again for she expects you. Savour every moment for it will be the last time that you will see her. It is nearly time for you to return to your homeland, but before you depart, I would like you to meet another lady, the Countess of Propriety, who resides in an ancient castle with the Count and nine children. Follow the river. It is not too far from the castle of the Red Queen. Now take off your breastplate and leave it here. If anyone asks you to divest yourself of any more armour except myself, you must refuse. Only I know when the time is ripe.

As soon as our young knight takes off his breastplate, the servant enters and gently leads him through the door to the outside. *You will no longer need to come here again. I wish you farewell and good fortune for your further endeavours. Your uncle blesses you.*

That evening he goes to visit the Queen with an intensity of conflicting emotions – joyfulness at the thought of being in her company again but desperate sadness knowing this will be the last time he will see her.

That night is to be the happiest of his young life. It starts however with much hilarity on their part because their young guest appears before them with only half his armour on – his helmet, leg and arm coverings and undergarment. *"Take off what's left of your armour and enjoy the dancing!"* they cry. *"I can't. The time has not come yet".* *"We think you're quite mad but we all love you!"*

The time comes when he has to depart, despite all their protestations. His voice has told him that he must arrive at the other castle at dawn so he must follow the river by night to get there in time. The Queen raises his visor, kisses his moist eyes and gives him a silver bracelet. *Take this as a token of my love.*

He stumbles out into the night and makes his way westwards along the river. As the sky lightens in the East, he espies in the distance an ancient castle with countless turrets. *Please God, let there be no more mirrors!* As he approaches, the drawbridge is lowered, and he is greeted by a group of nine children who take him to their mother, the Countess. She is a tall, dignified-looking and dark-haired lady who shows no surprise at the way he is dressed. *Let me show you to your room. It is in the West Wing.* The young knight enters his room with great trepidation, and is relieved to see there are no mirrors.

For three days he stays in the castle and is allowed to explore many of its rooms. One is a large library containing countless scrolls; another has collections of minerals and bones. There is no feasting and dancing, no entertaining tales are told. However occasionally, sober music is to be heard, played by the children. Everywhere there exudes a quiet and calm atmosphere of studiousness and hard work. He cannot but admire the graciously ordered way the Countess runs her family and household. It has almost lulled him into sense of wanting to settle down and study and give up his quest. As soon as he has that thought, his voice tells him that it is now time to return to his homeland where more ordeals await him, but where also he will find what he is looking for.

Reluctantly, the half-dressed knight takes his leave. On his way back, he has a beautiful dream soaring through the heavens in the warm south. His voice now directs him, not to his native village but to a modest dwelling in the capital city. *You will recognise it by the hawk of gold perched on its roof.* There he has to pass through his Fifth and Sixth Trials. In the room where he sleeps, there are now just two mirrors. In the one he sees his reflection dressed in rags scrabbling for food in a rubbish heap. This mirror not only makes him experience his image's hunger but also an overpowering stench that wafts out to him. He turns round to the other mirror on the opposite wall where now he sees himself with a black body, and he feels intensely the hostile and fearful gaze of others who look upon him. In this suffocating atmosphere he cannot get any sleep. So he tries to leave the room but the door is locked. Then his voice says, *Take off your remaining armour, except your helmet, and leave it here. You will now find the door unlocked. I want you now to seek for a large underground hall with a domed ceiling which is in the middle of the city. Here many ailing knights are languishing, and here you will be faced with your seventh and last trial. Now go and may God protect you.*

Dressed now in only a grey undergarment with the helmet on his head, he wanders through the streets getting colder and colder as it is now autumn.

Eventually he finds the underground chamber and is let in by a woeful-looking and bedraggled knight who introduces him to his companions. Never before has he seen so many sad-looking creatures. Some are wandering up and down in a state of agitation; others are standing stock-still staring into space; and others are propped up on divans. Their swords and lances are bent and what armour they have on is rusting. The young knight is filled with compassion for their sorry state, but he wonders how on earth he is able to help them. His voice then says, *Be patient. It will take a long time. Listen to their stories and you will learn how they have become the way they are. Three in particular will be able to help you.*

Many weeks and months pass and our young knight is beginning to dread his last ordeal which he knows he has to face here. There is only one old and cracked mirror in the corner of the hall, which he has kept well away from. Then one day, his voice tells him to go and look into it. Expecting it to be his worst trial, he casts a nervous glance at it. But what he sees is not something terrifying, only confusing, - a rapidly changing kaleidoscope of images; some of them he thinks are of himself but because of the cracks he can't clearly make out his face. Others seem to be of different gods and goddesses who are being prayed to in a babble of tongues. The style of his clothes keeps changing and the surroundings he is in, also change, - from wild forests to strange triangular-looking buildings to huge columned edifices. Accompanying these images is a swirling maelstrom of thoughts and feelings which are so utterly different from anything he has experienced before. His head begins to throb with pain and giddiness overcomes him. All the props that kept him upright begin to fall away. Recovering from his swoon, his voice whispers gently, almost inaudibly, *This will be a continuing ordeal throughout your life, but help will come when you need it. Now take off your helmet. You will feel cold and exposed but rest assured. You will find warmth and comfort in the room below this hall for there are many ancient documents stored there which will give you signs as to what your next steps are to be.*

Worse than the cold is the feeling that he is now completely defenceless. It feels like everyone is staring at him and through him. He retreats to the room below and starts reading.

One afternoon, he nods off and has a terrifying dream. The two noble ladies that he met in foreign lands, and who have remained in his heart, turn into all-powerful distortions of themselves. The one dazzles him with hot blinding white light which makes him swoon in ecstasy; the other freezes him into stone. He then finds himself balancing on a tight rope, fearful of falling off to the left and being smashed on the rocks below, or falling to the right, fly off like a moth into the light. He wakes up in a sweat with the question, **Who can help me maintain my balance?** He continues to read voraciously, and another question forms itself in his mind, **Was it necessary to have lost the light we once were given and to have become frozen in darkness for a while,** *so that we rediscover it from within; and who or what is the turning-point of the world?*

More weeks pass. Our young knight, although he hasn't yet found answers to these questions, feels like they are warm and colourful bursts of light that erupt in the gloom of his soul. But there is one huge question that begins to trouble him, *How can I help all these ailing knights if I am not able to help myself? I have been trained to wield a sword to defeat the enemies without. What about the enemies within?*

As soon as he has asked that question, his voice speaks to him again, which it hasn't for some time. *Good. You have now asked the four questions that I have been waiting for you to ask. Now go and share your thoughts with the three knights whom you have got to know. They will not give you answers, but they will point you in the right direction, particularly the third and last one, who will in fact speak the least.*

The one knight that he feels closest to, on hearing about his recent adventures of the mind, starts to confide in him the ancient secrets of his knightly order, called the Bronze Order of the Rooster. While doing so, he visibly brightens up for he was one of the more morose of the knights there. Our young hero feels his mind expanding into far horizons - a feeling of exhilaration, the likes of which he has never experienced before. After telling him his motto, *Wake up!* The Knight of the Rooster dons him with a bronze-coloured robe.

The next friend on hearing about his discoveries, instead of engaging him in lengthy conversation, simply smiles and reveals to him in a story the secrets of his order, which is the Order of the Silver Dove. *These Eight Teachings will help you forge a true sword of the soul. Now depart in peace and let me give you this silver girdle to wear.*

The third knight, on listening attentively to his questions, simply says, *You will find the secrets of my Golden Order of the Eagle, and much more, in the Room of the Documents. Look at the one with the title of '1879.' Nobody ever looks at it because it sounds so uninteresting. I call it my Open Secret.* He then takes out a gold ring and places it on the young man's finger. His last words are: - *It has already begun to be revealed to you how you can enlarge your mind and heart. Now learn to fortify your Spirit and go out into the world, make these things known to those who desire to know, and bring new things into being that were not there before.*

The young man hurries down to the room and with trembling hands he opens the *Document 1879* and begins to read. For the next three hours, he is transfixed. The little bursts of light which he had been experiencing earlier, now come together to dance such patterns of beauty and significance that he wants to get up and dance himself.

The next day, his voice says to him, *Now you can leave this place. You are ready to live for a while in a beautiful hall in the country, not far from here. There you will learn the secrets of creativity together with others who have gone on journeys similar to yours. During this time untold blessings will bestowed on you, to prepare you for new challenges ahead.*

He takes his leave of his three special friends and all the others in that strange underground chamber, and vows to himself that he will never forget them, for in an extraordinary way, their sufferings have contributed to his own healing.

The next three years turn out in the way his voice predicted. After two years of blissful creativity and living life to the full, he knows he has to leave and venture forth on his own again, to prepare for his future task. He finds himself retracing the path he took six years previously to foreign lands but this time he has a purpose. Strangely he experiences 'echoes' of that previous time; he meets two women, who remind him of the ones he met earlier, but now in an older and wiser form; he faces similar difficulties with the language and the people, and when it is time to leave, he has the same glorious dream of the warm south. When spring comes he is drawn back to his homeland, not knowing what his next move shall be. His voice remains silent. It feels like another ordeal. He knows his time of formal learning is over. Where is he to serve? Then out of the blue an invitation comes for him to go a distant land overseas. He tries to convince himself that this is the right path for him to take, and he prepares for the long journey.

But at the last moment he falls ill and cannot go. Then his voice speaks at last, *Don't worry. Your life task awaits you in the north at the court of King Arthur. It is time you should learn the secrets of Merlin that belong particularly to this isle. He will be there to instruct you.*

As soon as he is better, with mounting excitement he sets off on the road northwards. He is led to a big city. He is confused and surprised for he was expecting it to be near the sea. But here it is – a castle called Tintagel set in beautiful grounds, and the sea nowhere in sight. And there is a strange and intriguing-looking building next to it, named after Merlin.

He is given a warm welcome by all the inhabitants of the castle. Then Arthur looks at him severely and says, *"Are you prepared for the challenges ahead, for there will be many? Our motto is 'Know Thyself.'* The young man stutters, *"I hope...."* At that moment, Merlin interrupts him and says with a smile, *It is also 'And thou wilt know the World'.* Then together Merlin and Arthur chant, *Know the World, and thou wilt know thyself!* Then Merlin says, *I will teach you the secrets of the rocks and trees. For surrounding us is a wondrous land of hills and dales. You were wondering where the sea is. That is it, - now frozen into the folds of the land!* And he laughs uproariously. Pointing to the strange-looking building next door, he then says in a mysterious voice, *And in my cave, I will reveal to you the arts of my white magic.* Suddenly at that moment everything gets swallowed up in a sea mist.

Did you know the Merlin Theatre is going to be re-opened soon? His wife has just come into the room. The old man wakes up with a smile, and he looks at his watch. He has been asleep for five minutes.

The author welcomes feedback and comments from readers, please contact him on:
robertchamberlain43@outlook.com